ALSO BY GAYLE BUCK

LOVE'S MASQUERADE
(Best New Regency Author 1986, Romantic Times Reviewers Choice Award)

THE DEMON RAKE

LORD JOHN'S LADY
(Best Regency Novel 1988, Romantic Times Reviewers Choice Award)

THE RIGHTEOUS RAKEHELL

WILLOWSWOOD MATCH

A REGENCY CHRISTMAS
(coauthor, with Anita Mills, Patricia Rice, Mary Balogh and Edith Layton)

HONOR BESIEGED

HEARTS BETRAYED

MUTUAL CONSENT

THE WALTZING WIDOW

A CHANCE ENCOUNTER

HOW TO
WRITE
AND MARKET

THE
REGENCY
ROMANCE

BY
GAYLE BUCK

REGENCY PRESS
1991

Published by Regency Press
P.O. Box 2306
Bandera, Texas 78003

Cover design by Gayle Smith Advertising Design
Printed in the United States of America

Library of Congress Catalog Card Number: 91-61247
ISBN 0-9629423-0-8

10 9 8 7 6 5 4 3 2

For additional copies of HOW TO WRITE AND MARKET THE
REGENCY ROMANCE, complete the order form at the back of this book or
write to Regency Press at the address above.

CONTENTS

This book is dedicated to my husband,
whose help and encouragement made it possible.

DISCLAIMER

This book is designed to provide information about the subject matter covered. It is sold with the understanding that the publisher and the author are not engaged in rendering legal, accounting or other professional services. If legal or other expert assistance is required, the services of a competent professional should be sought.

The author and Regency Press shall have neither liability nor responsibility to any person or entity with respect to any loss or damage caused, or alleged to be caused, directly or indirectly by the information contained in this book.

INTRODUCTION

As the author of ten regency romances, I have often been asked questions about my writing: Where do you get your ideas? How can you sit down and actually write for 300 pages? Don't you ever run out of ideas? What do you do about writer's block? What is a regency romance? How much money do you make, if you don't mind saying? Do you have an agent? How did you find a publisher? How did you get published? How did you become a writer? When did you decide to become a writer?

The last two questions are easiest answered. After weighing some career options, I decided to become a writer in the fifth grade. From there on out I geared everything I could toward the goal that I had set for myself. First, I started to write. I wrote a decent short story for assignment in the sixth grade. I kept a notebook of scribblings and I read everything that I could get my hands on, both fiction and nonfiction.

When I was fifteen, I started the first novel that I ever finished. It was a regency.

This was no accident. I had discovered the books of Georgette Heyer the previous summer and had fallen in love with the regency era. I loved the pace of the books, the swift repartee, the romance, and the consummately drawn historical background of the period that was found between their covers.

Before I left high school, I had researched the publishing industry enough to know a little bit about how the money was made and who made it, the different genres on the market, and what the chances for new authors were in breaking into print.

What I discovered was that I had chosen a tough field.

It isn't easy to break into print. It takes a combination of talent, hard work, constant study and the willingness to learn, and a liberal dash of luck. It also takes the sort of determination that, even though it may become ragged before all is done or said, remains deeply entrenched. Some call this obstinacy of the worst kind. Others call it sheer stupidity.

Whatever, the first requirement towards becoming a successfully published writer is to never, ever give up on the dream. The second requirement is to write-and-submit, write-and-submit. The third is to grow a very thick skin as protection against the blows of heavy and constant rejection. The fourth is to resign yourself to others' well-meaning advice to get into something at which you can make a real living.

Writing a book is not a get-rich venture. You must expect to invest a lot of time and effort to ever even get a chance at catching a publisher's interest. Once you do so, however, don't be too disappointed when you are not offered a $500,000 contract. That sort of deal makes the newspapers because it is exceptional in any genre.

This book is designed to provide information about how to write for the regency romance genre. It is not a definitive work. There are always other sources to consult, especially for answers to questions about legal and other professional services. If legal or other expert assistance is needed, please do seek out a lawyer who is familiar with publishing contracts, for instance, or a literary agent whose speciality lies in the romance markets. This book is as thorough and accurate as possible within its scope, and hopefully will encourage you to learn as much as you can about not only writing but the publishing industry in general.

When I decided to write for the regency romance genre, there was no source book that I could go to that would show me how. What I know now about writing the regency romance I learned through trial and error, study and research. There are a lot of good how-to-write books out there, but none that are specifically geared toward someone who wants to try her hand in this very special genre. This book will hopefully make it easier to write and market your own work.

The Regency period in England was quite a different sort of historical period. The licentious days of *The Three Musketeers* had drawn to a close and the very correct Victorian Age had not yet begun. The short span of the Regency, all nine years of it, was something of a cutting edge in British history. In some respects the regency era was more modern than either the age that preceded it or the one that followed.

Some expert observers of history have noticed that changes in fashion are often a unique sign of social upheaval or evolution. During the regency era, women dispensed with the wide heavy panniers of their grandmothers and Marie Antoinnette. The fashionable dress was lightweight and figure-skimming, sometimes of such fine fabric that the entire garment could be pulled through a gold wedding band.

The society that approved of such freedom from repressive style for their women was equally liberal in its adjustment to new ideas and new movements in social structure. This is not to say that all was a bed of roses. Far from it. Any adjustments in society are accompanied by painful rites of passage. However, the regency era was unique in that the new and the old, the latter of which was personified by the world of the aristocracy, managed to exist side by side.

It would not be until the Victorian Age that the tightly corseted silhouette would come into vogue. The tumultuous adjustments of the regency era would quietly be replaced by an established order in which men's trousers were referred to as Unmentionables and piano legs were covered with skirts. The middle class would be firmly settled in place, and the aristocracy that had been would never be again.

The regency romance is good fun. If you have not yet read any, do so. There are many excellent regency writers on the market today. Certainly read Georgette Heyer's books. She was the one who actually established the regency as a separate genre. Also read Jane Austen, whose life encompassed the Regency and whose books were written about characters based on her contemporaries.

This book is meant as a guide of sorts. I have brought together elements that I think important in putting together the successful regency romance, as well as some insights about marketing. Needless to say, much of what is discussed is readily applicable to other genres - such things as plotting, character development, the use of description, etc. In fact, I realized to my astonishment that many writing techniques are useful across the board, whatever the genre, but the emphasis on one or another shifts depending on the type of book. However, other elements, such as the characteristics that make a regency romance different from any other historical romance, are unique.

The questions posed at the beginning are addressed in this book.

The viewpoint is mine, most of the experiences are mine. I enjoyed writing this book, and I hope that you derive as much enjoyment out of reading it. I also hope that these next pages prove of such use to you, both in your writing and in encouraging you to consult other sources, that a year from now there will be yet another regency romance writer on the bookshelves.

Chapter One

CHARACTERISTICS OF A REGENCY ROMANCE

Characteristics of the regency romance will be mentioned throughout the rest of the book, but I would like to begin with an overview here.

1) The regency romance is above all a tale of romantic entanglements and love. The story always has a happy ending, leaving the reader satisfied that, despite all former complications and misunderstandings, the heroine and the hero enter their future life together hand in hand and with shared laughter.

2) The regency romance is set against the glittering backdrop of English high society during the Regency, which spanned the years 1811 to 1820. The location of the story may be other than the city of London but the essential background - the British aristocracy - always remains the same.

3) The hero is an established member of the aristocracy. He is usually a peer in his own right or the heir to a title. He may be a member of the diplomatic service or of the military.

4) The heroine may be a member of the aristocracy. She also may be the daughter of a respectable family, her father a minister or a military man or the local squire. She may also be the daughter of a very wealthy tradesmerchant. Whatever the heroine's origin, she must always possess the

graces and the education that will suit her to become the wife of a peer and an accepted member of high society.

5) The regency romance tends to be a "comedy of manners". Social conventions play an important role in providing awkward circumstances and pitfalls for the heroine and the hero.

6) The regency romance often contains exchanges of strong wit and repartee between the characters. These exchanges highlight the personalities and opinions of the characters, as well as their sense of humor. Humor is often used to illustrate an evolution of the romantic relationship.

7) The regency romance often has idiosyncrasies or quirks of plot. Humor, mystery and suspense are used to spice the main story of romance, many times in the shape of sub-plots.

8) The regency romance showcases strong secondary characters. The supporting characters provide many of the complications that beset the heroine and the hero. Their roles range from the humorous to the villainous.

9) The regency romance relies heavily on careful and in-depth research. Perhaps more than any other genre, the regency romance can be made or broken by the authenticity of its historical detail. Accurate depiction of the setting is vital to the ultimate success of any regency romance because the readership is knowledgeable and vocal.

Through thorough research of the Regency period, the writer develops a pretty fair notion of the people and the time and can be fairly confident of passing the scrutiny of devoted regency romance readers. Once this is accomplished, it is time to mesh that knowledge with what is required of a regency romance by publishers.

Following chapters will deal in-depth with the setting, the heroine and the hero, secondary characters and plot. These all examine essential characteristics that are required in this genre. Other characteristics of the regency romance that must be dealt with are sex, social reform, religion and social customs. Publishers' guidelines touch on any or all of these topics, but sometimes in such a general and vague manner that the writer has to read through the lines.

Generally, sex in the regency romance is kept off center stage. Sex does take place between married couples, or a gentlemen and his mistress, but rarely does it include graphic description. No pornography, no crude slang names for anatomical parts, no disappointing lack of orgasm, no rape or brutality.

This is romance, which means that everything is blushing roses and golden haze and tumbling emotions. This is the kind of reading that gives a nice feeling, a pleasurable *frisson* up the spine, a catch of the breath. Lead up to a love scene gracefully, begin it, and pull back a little to allow the reader to form her own interpretations of your scintillating description.

None of this means that the lovemaking in the regency romance is without intensity. There is always tension between the heroine and the hero, whether of the man/woman kind or the anger of antagonists or the laughter of friends. Recall that this is a developing relationship and that the gradual progress culminates in a happy ending. Sex is not the ending. It is the binding. Lovemaking without laughter or tenderness or kindness is reduced to sterile description and uninvolved rutting.

The heroine of a regency romance is rarely sexually active outside marriage. Unless she is a widow, she probably doesn't have any experience past stolen kisses and compliments breathed warmly against her ear. She quickly learns more from the hero, of course. She learns that a mere brush of his fingers across her cheek, or an ardent kiss that crushes her body close against his, causes very warm reactions within her.

The revelation of her own sexuality is one of the factors that the heroine must deal with. Instantly, she is thrown into personal conflict. She is a lady and ladies are cool, genteel, proper. A lady does not throw herself into the arms of a gentleman. A lady swiftly quashes any shocking liberties taken with her. And yet, her heart beats staccato whenever she catches sight of the hero. Her voice fails her when he looks at her..just so. Her breath catches when he closes in on her. Ultimately, she is completely at his mercy when he takes her into his arms.

As for the hero, he is much more experienced than the heroine. He has probably kept a mistress or two over the years, or even have been married at one time. He knows the social taboos, but there is something about the heroine that drives him past the point of propriety. He is not content with a glance from her sparkling eyes or with circling her about the dance floor. He wants much more, and unless he is a confirmed and unscrupulous libertine, his personal conflict arises in that he must somehow maintain his distance.

The hero may be discovering that his hard heart is softening and that he is becoming vulnerable to the heroine. He fears that vulnerability, yet at the same time he cannot deny his feelings. He is finely caught and it angers and bewilders him. He realizes that to save himself he must somehow eradicate the heroine's hold upon his heart, but that proves impossible and in the end he admits to his love for her. In the meantime, though, the hero does take shocking liberties with the heroine. He kisses her, caresses her, brings them both to the flaring of passion. He simply cannot help himself, even if he fiercely maintains to himself and others that she is nothing to him.

All of this tension and passion is never seen by the circles of society that the heroine and the hero frequent. Public demonstrations of affection were considered outrageous at the time. If an unmarried young lady was seen clasped in the arms of an unmarried gentleman, then the gentleman was honor-bound to offer for the young lady so that her reputation would not be sunk beyond reproach. A young lady discovered in so intimate a pose could expect that society would forever blackball her and that her matrimonial chances had disappeared. Therefore, the kisses and caresses and whatever other liberties the hero attempts with the heroine have the fear of discovery attached to them.

The publishers' guidelines on sex within the regency romance can basically be reduced to this, then. The heroine is generally not experienced, unless she is a widow. She is not sexually active in the course of the book, unless she is married to the hero. The hero is an experienced lover, but even though he might desire the heroine he attempts to maintain a proper distance. He may take liberties with the heroine. If he is married to her, he does make love to her; but actual sex is left off center stage and much to the reader's imagination. Tension between the heroine and the hero is paramount to the successful telling of the regency romance, whether it is sexual tension or arises from some other source which impacts upon the heroine and the hero.

Now that I have said this, I want to point out exceptions to the above rule. Regency romances in the past few years have changed, most pointedly in the areas of sensuality level and the length of the book. Publishers who put out longer versions of the regency romance are amenable to more emphasis placed on sex, much in the style of other historicals. These longer regencies do sometimes place sex center stage.

The longer versions also have the more somber aspects of sex included within the stories - rape, incest, brutality. However, these more somber aspects are always treated as problems that the heroine must overcome. These happenings are usually part of the heroine's past and as such bring along with them mental and emotional baggage that make for further difficulty, or personal conflict, before the heroine is able to place her trust in the hero. Mary Balogh has written at least one regency romance that touches on the effects of this sort of sensuality.

Social reform will be touched on elsewhere, but I wish to add a few comments regarding it. In the longer regencies, along with the change in sensuality level, comes also a stronger emphasis on social reform or social questions. Some writers of the longer regencies use this format to present serious matters not often dealt with in romances. For instance, *The Rake and the Reformer* by Mary Jo Putney deals with alcoholism as a central element to the story. The regency period was a time of strong and frequent drinking. Wine was served at nearly every meal and on most social occasions. It was not uncommon to have drunken individuals staggering about the social functions. The hero in this particular story is an alcoholic and the heroine is the individual who encourages him to reform and to overcome his problem.

It is quite easy to understand that the longer regency romances that deal with these kind of issues are not as breezy as the classic regency. Their tenor is more somber. There is not the fun or the suspense that is the hallmark of the regency genre. If not carefully done, the romance itself can be completely overshadowed by the issue that the writer is dealing with. It is perhaps one of the most difficult feats to accomplish: presenting a serious issue in a constructive manner and yet maintaining a satisfying romance between the heroine and the hero.

None of this is to say that the longer regency romances are all of a more somber tone. Judith McNaught, though a writer of historicals, has also traveled into the regency period in some of her work. Her books are spirited and fun, and form a good example of what can be done with a longer work when humor is a primary ingredient.

Another element that should be dealt with when looking at the regency period, or indeed, very nearly any historical period of Europe, is religion. Since 800 A.D., when Charlemagne was crowned Christian Emperor of the Holy Roman Empire, all of Europe has been intimately influenced by the Roman Catholic Church. Daily life revolved about the Church in some form or fashion, as did the arts and government.

King Henry VIII of England had a falling out with the Pope and the Church over the question of setting aside one of his wives so that he could take another. Of course, being the determined gentleman that he was, he established his own church with himself at its head. This was the Anglican Church and though Roman Catholicism remained alive in England, the Anglican denomination was predominant in England at the time of the regency period.

Though usually religion is kept in the background as much as any other social aspect of the regency period, the Anglican Church does play a small part, to a greater or lesser degree, in the regency romance. Religious gatherings were as much for spiritual benefit as they were for socializing. Church-goers met their social peers at the cathedral or at the chapel on Sundays. Ladies compared their various outfits and progeny; gentlemen talked of politics or breeding their hounds. The first overture of a possible matrimonial match could be made while strolling with a particular young lady along the lane after the service let out. Various social functions that revolved around the church were important: christenings, the reading of banns for an engaged couple, the weddings, the funerals, the holiday festivities.

The concept of Christian charity was very much a part of the people's lives. In fact, the evangelical movement was quite strong during the era. This element actually gave rise to the beginning of the various social reforms that have their roots in the regency period and which showed such great social force later during the Victorian age.

Christian charity also showed strongly in various British traditions, such as the obligation that master and mistress had to see to the education and the welfare of the tenants who worked and lived on their estate. It was not only the landed peers and gentry who contributed to the welfare of those about them, but the vicar and his family, as well as various other members of the community, who took it upon themselves to offer aid to families less fortunate or to the sick and elderly. Alms were given to the poorhouse, as well as clothing and other necessities. Contributions, whether monetary or in the form of new roofing or the embroidering of altar cloths, were made to the local church or chapel.

The holiday season in particular had its traditions. For instance, Boxing Day, which fell on the first week-day after Christmas, was an event when all of the servants were given a personal present by the master or mistress of the house. An open-house was often held during the month in which the Christmas season was celebrated and oftentimes the guests included not only the usual social circle, but those who would not normally be invited to a private dinner party.

All of these things impact on the heroine and the hero in the regency romance. Perhaps one or neither is a particularly religious individual, but yet they will adhere to the various obligations and traditions of their culture and of their social background. This was called *noblesse oblige*.

The degree to which the element of religion appears in the regency romance depends on the attributes assigned to the characters and the particular plot of the book. Special licenses were granted by the Archbishop of Canterbury, and no runaway marriage was possible without it. The question of personal convictions, or faith, is an important one to decide for the heroine and the hero, even for the secondary characters or the villain. Especially if the heroine is the daughter of a vicar, she may be expected to have a firmer faith than another young lady who was brought up in the lap of luxury without a thought spent on anything but the next party. The heroine's personal code will have a direct impact on how she receives any offer of marriage, or an offer made by a libertine.

Regardless, the element of religion should be seriously considered as a strong source of personal conflict for either the heroine or the hero, or conflict between the heroine and the hero. This is especially true if the writer chooses to submit a proposal to a publisher that has a line that reflects religious social values. There are several publishers that offer such fiction lines. They include Harvest House Publishers, Regal Books, MacMillan, Bethany House Publishers, Harper's Library of Biblical Fiction (Division of HarperCollins), Zondervan, Crossway Books (Division of Good News Publishers), Word Publishing, Living Books, Harper & Row, David C. Cook Publishing, InterVarsity Press, Jove, and Bantam. Some of these publishers are not listed in the *Writer's Market*, (the large annual reference of publishers, etc.), but their addresses can be found on the flyleafs of the books at the local Christian bookstore. Several different historical periods are represented, though at present there does not appear to be one set in the Regency.

Religious social values will play a greater role in determining character conflict and motivation in books published by these lines. However, these considerations are also found in more secular lines. For instance, the following example of character conflict could work equally well for either type of publisher.

If the wealthy and nobly born hero, who is hard-hearted and cynical, is in pursuit of a young lady who is firm in her convictions, he could very well discover that his efforts to make her into his mistress are made that much more difficult. He must examine his own spiritual beliefs and morality in the light of his own reluctantly-born love for the heroine, and his eventual desire to make her, not his mistress, but his wife. As for the heroine, she is torn by the knowledge that the hero desires her physically, but he cares nothing for her mind or her emotional attributes. The heroine might discover that the hero is disguising his vulnerability of heart behind a hardened facade. She is drawn to him for that very reason and it is her own strength of character, her compassion and her kindness that eventually convince him that love can be true and all-encompassing.

Besides holiday traditions and customs, there are several social customs that were in vogue during the regency period, with only slight modifications from previous decades and which were continued into the Victorian era.

Hand-kissing had become less common by the regency period and was perceived as an intimate salute by a young lady. The gentleman was more proper in his salute by simply carrying the lady's fingers to his lips and brushing them with a polite pressure.

Morning and afternoon calls were embarked on by both sexes. These were formal visits to the residences of friends and acquaintances. The fashionable gentlemen made the rounds of various drawing rooms in order to discharge social obligations to various hostesses, or to meet a particular young lady in a more intimate atmosphere, or to form appointments with male acquaintances for different entertainments.

A gentleman could call informally on a friend in the morning and wait on his host while the valet helped his master on with his coat or join his host for breakfast, before they sauntered off together to Tattersall's to bid on horses. In the afternoon, the same gentleman could send his card in at a lady's residence and be formally received in her drawing room. The lady was rarely alone, having either a chaperone with her or other visitors.

The ladies also spent a great part of their time exchanging visits with other ladies. This social activity was a way to become better acquainted with new friends, to solicit the favor of someone's presence at an upcoming function, to hear the latest gossip, or to form commitments to go shopping together. A lady never called upon a gentleman at his personal residence, however. This was tantamount to declaring that she was fast and beyond common decency and that she was the gentleman's mistress.

Gentlemen and ladies both carried calling cards which were inscribed with their names and their addresses. These were left with servants whenever they called on an acquaintance who happened to be out. Calling cards were also inserted into letters or could be slipped into a posy of flowers or a box of sweets, as well. A personal note could be scribbled on the back of the card.

Tea was served formally at four o'clock in the afternoon. Often this was also a time when visitors would come by. Tea, biscuits, cake and fruit was served. The manner and graciousness with which the hostess or her deputy poured the tea was an indication of her good breeding or lack thereof.

Visiting the park was most advantageous to an individual's social reputation between the hours of five and six o'clock in the evening, as this was the time that the fashionable people chose to promenade, drive or ride. This was the time to be seen and to be recognized or even to be introduced to some fashionable hostess whose social gatherings were all the rage, or to catch the eye of some particular gentleman.

During the course of a London social function, dinner was served very late by present standards. Nine or ten o'clock was not unusual. Afterwards, dancing and card-playing continued until three or four o'clock in the morning. In the country, "town hours" were often not adhered to and dinner was served at the early hour of six o'clock.

A dinner party could literally go on for five to eight hours. It is mind-boggling to think of the guests sitting at table for hours at a time as they were served course after course after course. The letters of Jane Austen and memoirs by others casually describe such marathons as unexceptional.

Bond Street and St. James Street were strictly off limits to the ladies. This fashionable area was the gentlemen's territory. Ladies never drove down or walked down these streets, whether or not they were alone, because to do so would excite unwelcome attention and label them as shameless and fast.

The waltz was introduced in 1812 by Countess Dorothea Lieven and Lord Palmerston at Almacks'. Before this fashionable debut, the dance was considered to be fast and shocking.

Almacks', the fashionable Assembly Rooms in King Street off St. James Street, was the most exclusive social club in London. It was the brainchild of seven prominent London hostesses, most of whose ages in 1814 are noted. Mrs. Drummond-Burrell, 28, and Lady Castlereagh were described as *grandes dames*. Lady Sally Jersey, 28, was the most hated because "her bearing was that of a theatrical tragedy queen". She was also noted for a saucy tongue and needle wit. Young and beautiful at 27, Lady Emily Cowper was the most popular hostess. Princess Esterhazy, 20, was called a *bon enfant*. Countess Dorothea Lieven, 30, was haughty and exclusive. She was the Russian ambassador's wife and delighted in political intrigue. She and Lady Jersey disliked one another "most cordially". Lady Maria Sefton was kind and amiable.

Almacks' success did not rest either on its entertainment or its refreshments. Until the introduction of the waltz, which infused the gatherings with some excitement, the norm were sedate country dances. The refreshments served consisted of lemonade, tea, bread and butter, stale cake and wafer-thin slivers of ham.

The real draw of Almacks' was its exclusivity. In order to pass through the doors, special vouchers of admission were required. These vouchers were dispensed by the seven hostesses only to those who were deemed to be of sterling quality within the ranks of society. Once denied vouchers to Almacks', a lady or gentleman was considered to be a degree beneath the socially elite.

Almacks' was the place to see and be seen. The most eligible bachelors in England could be certain to make an appearance there. As a result, every socially ambitious mother schemed to gain the favor of one of the seven patronesses in order to receive one of the coveted vouchers for her daughter. Georgette Heyer called Almacks' the "Marriage Mart", and so it was.

Regency romances share many of the same characteristics of other historicals. However, basic differences can be found.

The regency romance setting is more anchored. Though sometimes the story is set outside of England, the British aristocracy is always the primary background ingredient and that fact narrows the number of possible geographical locations. Other historical romances are set very nearly anywhere in the world and in any time. In fact, even within the scope of a single historical romance, the heroine and the hero's story can bounce from Europe to the American coast to the Caribbean and back again. The heroine and the hero thus deal with several different settings and social cultures within one book. In these books the setting is often not nearly as important as the romance. In a regency, the era itself almost takes on the aura of a separate character.

The regency romance will usually place more emphasis on character interchanges that highlight personality differences and the effects of skewed social conventions. Other historical romances place more emphasis on interchanges that create or illustrate sexual tension and lovemaking.

Historical romances taken as a whole are marketed from the standpoint of sex appeal. Examine several covers from different publishers and you will see that most of illustrations are of a half-undressed couple freeze-framed in a passionate clinch. The blurbs on the covers advertise "dark passion", "bittersweet love", "blazing passion", "tarnished ecstasy", etc. I have heard authors of historical romances express dissatisfaction that there is so much skin displayed on the covers because they feel that their books are about more than sex. However, writers have little, if any, control over what goes on the cover of their books.

The regency romance book cover is different. The heroine and the hero are positioned together, but they remain clothed. The blurbs are also different: "love's tables turned", "fair game", "love-shy young lady".

This difference in advertising points up the basic difference in the type of love story that the regency reader is buying. Since there is less sex on center-stage, the regency romance must rely on other elements like the "comedy of manners" to create a wonderful love story. The ongoing steady life of the genre, whose roots can be traced to the regency era itself through Jane Austen's legacy, illustrates its ever-present popularity.

Chapter Two

THE PLOT

Contrary to what many might assume, a plot is not static. The plot is a basic idea or outline, a body that must be allowed to change some part of its clothing when necessary.

The plot can be as simple as a one page description of the story or as involved as a ten page formal outline, like those that students in an English class are taught to put together for a research paper. Each writer experiments to find the technique that is most comfortable and most helpful to him or her.

My suggestion is to first write down as much as possible about the storyline that you have in mind, and every situation and snippet of conversation that you have imagined for your characters up to this point. Don't worry too much about the *form* of the outline. What is most important at this point is to get down the ideas that have inspired you. Then go back and rearrange or alter or enlarge upon as you think best. If you are more comfortable with a formal outline, by all means arrange it in this fashion. If you prefer a free-form prose description, then write it this way.

However you arrange it, this will be your rough outline. This is the plot that you begin with and that serves as your guide. When you actually start writing, the plot will usually take on a smoother shape, casting off certain accessories that turn out not to be as important as you had first assumed and putting on other accents that you may not even have dreamed of when the original ideas fired your imagination.

The worst mistake any writer can make is to expend more time and energy on developing a plot then on the actual writing of the story. Things happen while writing. Characters say or do unexpected things or the glimmer of a subplot suddenly surfaces. If the writer stifles these creative urges, then ultimately the story is not as good as it might have been. Indeed, an overdeveloped outline that is strictly adhered to despite the flashes of inspiration that come during the process of writing will actually cripple the story. This can easily mean the difference between fascinating or trite, sale or rejection.

Plotting is usually one of the most difficult areas for any writer to master. Much of what is learned is by trial and error and through instinct - what realistically works and what doesn't in capturing the reader's belief in the story.

However, there are techniques that can be zeroed in on that will be of help in developing the plot. The tools that we will touch on are: coincidence, tension, conflict, character motivation, fatal flaw, foreshadowing, and cause-and-effect.

Coincidence is defined as "a remarkable occurrence by chance". Please reread that statement, noting particularly the words "remarkable" and "chance". Whatever is to occur must be remarkable in the context of the story and must happen by chance.

The effective use of coincidence can enhance the plot, given certain circumstances. Use coincidence to set up a plot complication. What the characters do thereafter with the information or the circumstances provided by the coincidence will move the story along, as well as provide added tension or a new plot twist, or even a sub-plot. (Sub-plots are wonderful tools in themselves, providing greater complications or misunderstandings, and depth, both to the characters as well as to the overall story.)

Coincidence also works as a technique for plotting when the situation described seems so bizarre or contrived that it is unbelievable, until later story events proved that the coincidence is actually a logical happening. Then the reader can accept the contrivance as a well-fitted puzzle piece where before it seemed totally off-key.

Humor is a wonderful conveyor of coincidence. If the coincidence is outrageous and blatant enough that the reader realizes that it is deliberately done, then the reader is quite willing to laugh and accept the coincidence at its face value. For example, the heroine and the hero each have a previous love-interest. When they fall in love with each other, one of the difficulties of the story is what to do with their former fiances. The heroine and the hero are in a quandary over how to let these other characters off gently and plan elaborate schemes for the purpose. They are startled and amazed when their former fiances suddenly elope together to Gretna Green. At one stroke, through blatant coincidence, the original problem is solved. But...what about those elaborate schemes that have been put in motion? Surely there are consequences, and probably humorous ones, at that.

Coincidence will not work if it's sole purpose is to resolve plot difficulties. This is a very important point. If the writer cannot think of a plausible way to save the characters from what seems a fool-proof trap or come up with a plausible ending, then the use of coincidence becomes very tempting. For example, the heroine is accidently locked in the hero's wardrobe where she conceals herself to avoid being caught in his bedroom. (I have no idea why she is there - a rather intriguing situation in itself.) The heroine cannot suddenly recall that she has the key to the wardrobe in her pocket, unlock it from the inside and coolly go about her business. Do not succumb to this form of coincidence. If events do not arise logically out of earlier events or through the actions of the characters, then the reader will not buy the story. Literally, the story will not be bought. Remember, the story is read first by an editor, who decides whether the story is marketable.

Coincidence is a useful and effective plotting tool when it moves the story along. However, if the coincidence threatens the believability of the story for the readers, then it must be deleted.

The structure of a story is called the plot. Plot is made up of scenes. How these scenes are interconnected, or the sequence of events, determines the richness, the tension, and the believability of the story.

Tension is the ongoing thread that will draw the reader from beginning to end. Tension is created through action, (or interaction, if you will). A scene is always action-oriented. The action can be physical, such as a horse race, or a duel, or it can be verbal, such as an argument between the heroine and the hero. Whether physical or verbal, the action is always acted out.

The scene whose sole purpose is to air the heroine's inner reflections and nothing else is one-sided and boring. Instead, as the heroine reflects, give her something to do, such as arranging the flowers for that evening's ball. Naturally, her thoughts must at some point gravitate to what she is doing. Perhaps she is thinking unkindly of the hero and the fight they have had and she discovers that she has so viciously jammed the stems of the roses into the vase that she has broken them. This small bit of action points up the heroine's extreme displeasure with the hero and her subsequent disgust with herself at ruining the roses highlights another facet of her personality.

There should be a point to each scene. The physical action or verbal interchange can remain unresolved at the end, but whatever occurs must have an impact later in the story. This impact can be the seed of a new plot complication or can lead the characters to act in a certain way when next they meet.

The conflict within the scene creates tension, which automatically heightens reader interest in what is going to happen next. The conflict also helps the writer to decide where to take the story next. This spurs the sequence of events that must logically lead to an inevitable and satisfying conclusion.

Creating conflict is not as difficult as some might think. Simply put an obstacle into the character's path. Tell the character that he can't have what he wants. The character must react because that is the human thing to do.

For example, the hero is an arrogant rake who is used to having any woman he wants fall willingly into his arms. He decides that he wants the heroine. He asks for an introduction to her, but his hostess refuses his request because she doesn't want to be the one to expose the heroine to this libertine. The hero is angered, not only by the obstacle placed in his path but by the hostess's stinging assessment of his character. Now added to his original desire to become known to the heroine is the need to prove that simply having his acquaintance will not ruin the young lady. The hero flies against convention and creates a minor scandal by introducing himself to the heroine.

The heroine has already been warned against this rake. Also, she is all too aware of the stares and the whispers that the rake's attention is garnering. She declines his invitation to dance with him, not only to preserve her social standing but to serve the hero a setdown for his arrogant assumption that he had only to hold out his hand to her for her to fall in with his wishes.

The hero is exceedingly angered now. He has been balked twice, once by the hostess and once by the heroine. He becomes even more determined in his pursuit of the heroine. His initial attraction to the heroine has been altered. His ego and his reputation demand that he make an impression upon her.

Continued tension and conflict are created by telling your characters that they can't have what they want over and over. The characters then are forced to work out ways that they will be able to attain their goals or desires. In the example above, the hero lays siege to the heroine's defenses. The story becomes one of light skirmishes between the hero and the heroine, and the unfolding of the obstacles that are placed in the hero's way by social conventions, well-meaning friends and acquaintances, and the heroine's protective relations. Certainly not least of the obstacles that the hero encounters and must overcome is the heroin's wary heart.

Some writers are fortunate enough to have a story come to them full-blown and perfect in every detail. Most of us at some point come to a dead end in the story and sit staring at the page without a clue how to go on. What happens next? Answer that question and you've created another small but vital piece of the overall plot.

This is as good a moment as any to address the very real problem of writer's block, because it is often associated with formulating the plot. Every writer , published or not, experiences writer's block at one time or another; some more than others.

True writer's block is caused, I believe, by stress.

Every profession or avocation carries the potential of burn-out. The corporate world talks about executive burn-out. Students become burned out. Burn-out is a condition in which frustration and depression prominently figure; a condition that is directly attributable to overloads of stress.

Some interesting parallels can be drawn between burn-out and writer's block. Writer's block also includes feelings of frustration, (I can't write a single decent sentence!), and depression, (I'll never be a good writer/the writer I once was.) In addition, writer's block becomes self-perpetuating. If you feel that you can't write, then you don't write, and the period of writer's block, or nonproductivity, is extended.

Writer's block can be a deadly enemy, but it can be managed.

The first weapon to bring against writer's block is your pen. Write. It doesn't matter how badly your work stinks. Write. You are in a blue funk and every word you write is garbage. Well, my friend, it isn't true. You are in a peculiarly censorious state and therefore you are the person *least* qualified to judge the worth of your writing. Save every page of garbage, because eventually the writer's block lifts and you will not be so excessively judgmental. At that time you will discover that not everything you wrote was bad. You may even find one or two gems among all the rot that actually excites you. That's an awfully nice reward for making it through a bleak period.

The second effective weapon against writer's block is to vary your routine. Go for a long walk. Pet the dog or cat. (This is not so far-fetched as it sounds. Research has shown that stroking a pet is actually so soothing that in some instances blood pressure is lowered.) Indulge in a leisurely bath. Brew a cup of herbal tea. Try out that new exercise video. Bake some bread. Whatever you do, stop thinking about how awful your writing is going and concentrate on something outside yourself. Do not do anything that will have the effect of graying your mood. The whole purpose of varying your routine is to brighten you outlook.

The third weapon against writer's block is to make an attempt to reduce the stress. You have heard this before, I know, but it does have merit. A regular exercise program, balanced diet, and adequate rest are definitely helpful. A car does not perform at its optimum with its air intake restricted, on the wrong gas, and with a low battery. We need proper care, too. It makes sense to invest in ourselves. If your body is bankrupted, you cannot expect your mind to function creatively.

Some sources of stress are not so easily overcome. These include personal and familial illness or accident. The one serious period of writer's block I have experienced took place over a five-month period. I had the flue twice, my toddler was at home every day, all day, for ten weeks with excruciating and chronic constipation, and my other little boy had emergency surgery. In addition, there were the Thanksgiving and Christmas holiday commitments and the usual children's flu and infection season.

I had a deadline to meet. It was absolutely paralyzing to watch the days slip by without being able to see comparable progress with my book. Whenever I did manage to write a few pages, I castigated myself for not writing faster and better.

Fortunately my editor understood that it was impossible for me to make up for five lost months in the time remaining before my deadline. She agreed to a new deadline, bless her. However, the down side was that this delayed the publication date of the book by nine months.

I recently met a lady who lost her husband to a prolonged illness shortly after her book was accepted. The publisher wanted to extend a multiple-book contract to her, but she declined. She did not want to be locked into a contract deadline until she had taken a few months both to settle her husband's estate and to grieve for her loss. I respect this lady for her wisdom in refusing to place herself in a position that would be highly conducive to writer's block. By the way, the publisher had an option on her next work whenever it should be completed, so she was not left out in the cold.

There are two forms of writer's block that can often be sidestepped, or at least defanged. One is comparable to smashing into a wall - the story just won't go even though you know what comes next. The other is simply fear of the size of the project.

When I get stuck in the story, even though I know where I want to go, it is because I am trying to do something with the characters that my subconscious says is not right for the story. I have learned to back off from the scene that is giving me difficulty and to move on to another portion of the book. When I eventually return to the difficult scene, it usually falls into place with hardly a whimper. Invariably, however, my characters are doing or saying something, or even reacting, differently than I had supposed they would.

This has been a very valuable lesson to me as a writer.

Attempting to fight writer's block head-on is a battle already lost. Allow the writer's block to have the field - there is a reason for it. Give yourself time to work out what your subconscious has already sensed about that particular scene. Meanwhile, work on another portion of the book. There is no rule that states a book must be written in order: beginning, middle, and end. (However, when you do jump about like this, a story outline helps to remind you where the main road lies.) You will still be progressing with the story despite having come to a dead stop. When you are ready to tackle the problem-scene, it will go smoother than you anticipated and probably be better than it would have been in its original form.

The fear of the size of the project is fairly easy to deal with, as well. When you think about writing a 300-page book, the sheer number of pages required often overwhelms. The trick is to cut the project into more manageable portions. For example, three hundred pages can be divided into thirty ten-page chapters. Make a commitment to write one chapter a day. One chapter a day doesn't sound so bad, does it? In a month's time you will have the book completed. Breaking a project into manageable parts is a mental trick used by managers in the corporate world. It can work for the writer, as well. Of course, the example above does not take into account domestic crises, the other forms of writer's block, and rewrites; but nevertheless, a writing schedule with set and small, reasonable goals will be rewarded by steady progress.

When I spoke about the kind of writer's block that is caused by subconscious rejection of an intended scene, I neglected to point out a rather odd thing. This type of writer's block could very well be labeled a plotting tool, because the scene's original form is usually modified. Modifications always cause adjustments in plot.

Building a plot is a very individual thing. Each writer has his or her own technique. Some develop extremely detailed outlines, while others are inspired by a general theme. Kasey Michaels decides first what will be her heroine's strongest character attribute, such as impetuosity, and that serves as the seed from which the plot arises. Ms. Michaels literally weaves a plot around the heroine that will best reflect that one 'particular character attribute.

For myself, when I sit down to write a new story I usually have just a scene or two in mind and an overall setting. This is not really as unsubstantial as it sounds.

I know that the story is a regency romance. This gives me the historical time and setting, the background, the feel of the reality I want to create. This is true of whatever genre the writer wants to break into. Every genre has a certain feel, certain givens. Fantasy requires magic; science fiction requires believable technology in fantastic settings; men's adventure requires fast-paced bloody action; sagas require complicated relationships and dark secrets; glitz requires money, sex, and the ruthless use of power.

Regency romances require happy endings, so I know that the heroine and the hero end up together happily ever after. They become betrothed to one another or, if caught in a marriage of convenience, they pledge their newly-sprung love.

The few scenes that I have envisioned are usually ones of specific dialogue, of tension, of perhaps physical action. Through those scenes, I have already met my heroine and hero, so I have a fair idea of their personalities and their circumstances and I know what will motivate them. In short, I have the essence of the story.

Building on that essence, I must more narrowly define the characters. The characters must want something and there must be sides to their personalities that will delineate what they are willing or capable of doing to attain their goals. This also helps to delineate what can be included in the plot. Finally, there must be consequences: if the characters *do not* strive for their goal, then something specific happens; if the characters *do* strive to attain their desire, then something else happens. For example, if the heroine does not accept the first suitor who presents himself, then she is doomed to living in her lecherous step-father's house. If she does accept the first suitor, then she must accept a loveless marriage. If she turns to a childhood friend, who is himself seeking a certain kind of bride, then the heroine jumps into a fiery situation that has the potential to end happily.

The characters must have strong personality attributes that will give them the potential to overcome all obstacles on the way to attaining their goals. The heroine could be very obstinate. She will not accept her step-father's overtures; she will not wear a dowdy gown guaranteed to earn the

23

first suitor's approval; she will not be the obedient and comfortable wife that her childhood friend wrongly envisions that he wants.

This same obstinacy can also be used as the heroine's fatal flaw. She may be so insistent on her own way that she drives away the one gentleman who could make her the happiest. In this case, the heroine needs a counter-balancing trait that will enable her to curb her obstinacy whenever it threatens her own best interests. Whatever negative personality attributes that the character might possess, the character must also have a positive attribute that has the potential to overcome the fatal flaw, thus making possible the attainment of the character's ultimate goal.

Fatal flaws are essential in creating well-rounded, or human, characters. Total perfection in a character is admirable, but not many of us can easily relate to such a person. Besides, it is not logical that a character who is the persona of total perfection will do or say anything that will create conflict. A character that has no weaknesses or negative qualities does not easily fit into awkward situations and that limits the character's usefulness within the plot. Fatal flaws are also essential because these traits have a way of creating clashes between characters. This in turn creates new tensions and new obstacles, which deepens the architecture of the plot.

Another useful tool in plotting a story is foreshadowing. Foreshadowing tells the reader that something different is about to happen. It is a technique that creates anticipation and tension. The reader will be looking for something new to develop. The writer had better deliver.

Foreshadowing is a promise from writer to reader that must be kept. For instance, the hero encounters a particularly obnoxious fellow who boasts that he has the heroine eating out of his palm. Angered, the hero warns the smug and arrogant fellow that there better not be anything planned that will impugn the lady's honor. The fellow laughs and the hero is left with an uneasy feeling. The hero has therefore threatened the villain, and set out the guidelines under which that threat would take place. For no really good reason, the hero feels uneasy; this is foreshadowing. Later in the story, it is logical to follow up that uneasy feeling, and the circumstances that caused it, with just such a situation as the hero has warned the villain against. The villain places the heroine into a situation that threatens her physically or with negative social consequences; the hero steps in to soundly thrash the villain and save the heroine.

Foreshadowing can also be used as a red flag by the writer to herself. The writer may end a chapter with a bit of foreshadowing because it sounds good, without having the least clue of what is actually going to happen next. Since the writer must follow up with something to justify the foreshadowing, that nudge is oftentimes just enough to get the story rolling smoothly again. Foreshadowing hints at a subtle change in atmosphere or a new plot twist; it indicates the tone of the story that must be established in order to encompass the changes. Therefore, foreshadowing in and of itself can be used to further plot when the writer is at an impasse for ideas.

Foreshadowing can be used to clarify or highlight a particular theme of the story or to predict events that will plunge the characters into conflict. Also, foreshadowing can be used to introduce an object or a character that will have an important impact on the story later, such as the locket treasured by the heroine later turns up in the villain's coach and proves to the hero that the villain had something to do with the heroine's disappearance, or the disreputable woman that is shooed from the heroine's door is later revealed to be a friend of the heroine's old nurse, who is determined to convey awful tidings about the heroine's actual birth.

Foreshadowing can be overdone. Never end every or every other chapter with bold hints of things to come. Overuse of the technique anesthetizes the reader and kills whatever anticipation you are trying to build. Foreshadowing works well when placed in introductory pages and at third-way points throughout the story. This measured spacing keeps the reader's appetite whetted, without becoming too heavy-handed, and helps the writer keep track of where the story must go. It also unfolds the character's expectations and sustains the mood of the story.

The use of cause-and-effect are essential to plot clarity. For every cause, there is an effect; conversely, for every effect, there is a cause. For example, the hero steals a kiss from the heroine (cause); she slaps his face (effect). Why does the heroine react in this manner? The heroine despises the hero (effect), because she has heard of his reputation as a card-shark and she suspects that he is responsible for her brother losing a fortune at gaming (cause). Begin with the cause and you must provide an effect. If you have decided first what the effect is, (such as the heroine's state of mind), you must provide the cause for that effect.

Cause-and-effect are a logical progression of events. In the example above, show first in the story the heroine's discovery of her brother's ruin and the hero's influence upon that unfortunate event *before* the moment that the heroine slaps the hero's face. This makes the second event much more powerful and believable. It also makes possible a much richer scene of tension and conflict between the heroine and the hero, because without the background to explain the heroine's motives, there are only her confused feelings at the hero's outrageous overture. However, with the addition of the background, the heroine can accuse the hero of perfidy and get a fine argument rolling that must enhance the character's later interrelationship.

The sort of plot found in a regency romance is what is commonly referred to as "a comedy of manners". This is a lighthearted romance relying heavily upon the social conventions of the regency era to provide awkward situations and outrageous circumstances for the heroine and the hero to work their way through. Needless to say, humor is often a strong ingredient. Subplots or secondary characters provide much of the action.

This is not to say that more somber touches are not existent in these romances. The social problems of the day are remarked upon, but the main story-line is always acted out against the glittering life of the aristocracy and their idiosyncrasies.

There is a growing trend in regencies to deal more thoroughly with social disgruntlement and reform, with the war, the poor, and the problems of burgeoning industrialization. The longer regencies that are now published have greater scope and latitude for addressing these issues, without sacrificing the essential romantic and lighthearted character of this specialized genre.

How does the writer come up with a uniquely regency era plot? First, the essentials must be kept in mind: time frame, happy ending, and "comedy of manners". Then delve into your research, where you will probably be struck by an interesting fact that sparks a few ideas.

For instance, there was an actual Regency gentleman who collected snuffboxes. He had one for every day of the year, each one quite distinctive in design and quite valuable since they were of silver and gold and were decorated with precious stones, etc. Suppose the fictional hero collects valuable snuffboxes, and suppose that he stakes one in a losing wager. Suppose the snuffbox falls into the hands of the villainess, who uses it as evidence to convince the heroine that the hero has been in her boudoir. Some of the plot's complications would arise out of hero's efforts, first of all, to discover what the heroine is holding against him and, secondly, to clear himself.

Another example is taken from one of Emily Hendrickson's books, called *The Gallant Lord Ives*. In her research, Ms. Hendrickson discovered that the first submarine prototype was developed during the Regency and she was subsequently inspired to write about a hero who made use of a submarine. The result was a touch of high-tech, Regency style.

Interesting research is not the only source for plot ideas. Human reactions to certain events or circumstances is a timeless approach in developing plot. Consider Shakespeare's *Hamlet,* the prince who discovers that his mother and his step-father successfully conspired to murder his father. The play's plot revolves around the question of what Hamlet, who feels himself going mad, will do with this horrific discovery. Another example is Scarlett O'Hara in *Gone With the Wind*, who wants more than life itself to revive the destroyed plantation, Tara, to its former glory. Scarlett will literally go to any extreme to attain her goal, no matter who might suffer in the process. Her obsession eventually destroys the lives of those around her and drives away the one man who makes her happy. In the end, all she has left is Tara.

One last example, is from my own book, *Mutual Consent*. The heroine only agrees to wed a certain gentleman, whose gambling debts are held by her tyrannical father, because she hopes that the hero is strong enough to win freedom for them both from her father's dominance. It is an allegiance built on expediency that must somehow evolve into one of trust and love. The plot focuses on the developing relationship between the heroine and the hero, which to a certain extent hinges on the reason behind the heroine's oddly desperate determination to escape from her father.

Plot, then, can be composed from several components. Character, setting (research), a particular idiosyncrasy, peculiar circumstances - all may play a vital role in developing a good, readable book. How each writer perceives and pursues the components makes for unique and original storytelling. However, it is the techniques and tools of plotting - coincidence, tension, conflict, character motivation, fatal flaw, foreshadowing and cause-and-effect - that breathe life into the different components.

Once the plot components are meshed with the proper plot techniques and tools, the book takes on a genuine life of its own.

Chapter Three

CHARACTER CONFLICT

When creating character conflict in the regency romance, there are several basics to keep in mind.

Remember that this story is first and foremost a romance. There is room for other elements, such as mystery or suspense or humor, but these provide the background music.

The primary melody that will arise from between the covers of the book will be the establishment and the development of a romantic relationship between the heroine and the hero. These characters should be so finely drawn by the writer that their interactions will seem familiar to anyone who has ever been through the oft-wonderful and sometimes awful process of falling in love.

As in any relationship, there will be points of difference - of opinion, of upbringing, of moral beliefs, of personality. These differences will inevitably clash in some fashion, resulting in the conflict between characters that breathes life into these otherwise flat-dimensional creations. Each difference that is exercised between the characters must somehow be resolved, but with the result that the resolution leads to another and perhaps more serious conflict. Such escalation of conflict carries the reader from beginning to end without skipping a beat. Never allow the characters to be in total agreement (at least, not for long) until the very end. Only then can the characters, and the reader, be allowed to rest. If the writer does this, the book will be lively, entertaining and thoroughly engrossing.

Elements like humor and mystery and suspense serve to enhance the romantic thread that ties it all together. How you treat the addition of these elements is up to your own inclination. One of the earliest regency romances that used suspense and mystery to startling effect was Georgette Heyer's *Cousin Kate*. In this book, the romance is played out against a tale of madness and murder. Generally, it is best to use mystery and suspense in the guise of sub-plots. Often, as in *Cousin Kate*, sub-plots serve as excellent counter-points to the romance.

Humor can be used across the board, either to break the tension within the sub-plot or to give a romantic scene an extra twist. Humor can be accomplished by placing the characters in an outrageous situation and allowing them to react to it. Or humor can be carried onto the stage by a secondary character, whose presence also warrants a reaction from the main characters. (The reaction of the characters is actually a form of character conflict.) The heroine and the hero themselves can be the source of the humor through a sequence of witty repartee. In fact, this last is a hallmark of the regency genre.

Humor is perhaps one of the subtlest tools for crafting character conflict. At first glance, the characters are simply having fun. But always there is something else to be read between the lines. Perhaps the hero comes to have a greater appreciation for the heroine's swift mind, so much so that he becomes warier in his dealings with her. Perhaps the heroine discovers in the hero a previously hidden charm of personality, one that she is drawn to and that she initially feels is a threat to her untouched heart. Both of these examples can very well be derived out of a humorous situation or exchange and both set the characters up for future conflict or misunderstandings.

The romance plays against the backdrop of English high society during the Regency, which spanned the years 1811 to 1820. It is most important to remember this because a regency romance does not exist outside this specific milieu. Regency romances are read as much for the historical setting as they are for the romance.

This setting contributes many elements of the possible conflicts that may arise among the story's characters. These elements run the gamut from social convention to family expectations of the characters, to politics and everything in between. For instance, social conventions were somewhat rigid. A young lady would think twice before accepting a carriage ride from a gentleman. Even if the gentleman was well-known to her, she could run the risk of discrediting her reputation if someone was to observe her in the gentleman's company, unchaperoned. Does the heroine accept the risk? What is the hero's reaction, especially if he is not the gentleman who was kind enough to offer the heroine a ride? Another example could be the heroine's determination that she will not be left behind in England after the hero has been invited to join the staff of the allied armies stationed in Brussels in the months before the Battle of Waterloo. What is the reaction of the heroine's family? If she is married to the hero, what are his reasons for wanting her to stay behind and what are hers for wanting to go with him? Is it a marriage of convenience on the hero's part and a love match on the heroine's side?

Whatever was in common practice as far as social conventions went or whatever was happening in the world during the Regency can be used to create interesting situations for the characters. These situations will be the stuff that showcases the conflict between the characters.

The hero is almost invariably an established member of the aristocracy. The only exceptions I have seen to this rule have been an American-born hero, who travelled to London because he had inherited a title, and a hero whose maternal grandfather was a wealthy mill owner, but whose father happened to be the younger son of a peer. In this case, too, the hero was the heir to the title. One other exception comes to mind, and that is the younger son of a peer who had gone off to India and returned a very wealthy man. This hero was not heir to the title, did not want to be, and, even though he was welcomed with open arms, he detested the frivolity of society. Nevertheless, he did have an established place within the aristocracy.

I have not yet said anything about the heroine because she has far fewer social limitations placed upon her within the regency romance genre.

The breakdown of requirements for the heroine and the hero follow.

Heroine	Hero
Wealthy and nobly born	Wealthy and nobly born
Poor but nobly born	Poor but nobly born
Wealthy but of merely respectable birth	
Poor and of merely respectable birth	

The hero who is wealthy and nobly born is expected to contract an advantageous marriage that will further enhance his descendents' lineage as well as their finances.

The hero who is poor but nobly born must contract an advantageous marriage that will save the family from financial ruin. If the bride is also of good lineage, then so much the better.

Here are two distinctive heros. The first is established, confident in his wealth, and able to indulge himself however he pleases. He is able to put off marriage until a time when he must beget an heir, but otherwise he feels no need to bestir himself to the altar. His wealth and his lineage entitle him to privileges unbounded. His every whim is instantly catered to and his least desire can be had at the ordering. It would be wonderful indeed if his character is not corrupted to some degree by the adulation. More than likely he has, or has had, one or several mistresses through the years. He won't dabble in prostitutes, however, because readers prefer that the hero show that he has the capacity of being able to form a monogamous relationship with the heroine. He is sought after as a very eligible bachelor and he has all of society from which to choose his bride.

The second hero must marry, and marry well, or face dire consequences. The family home is mortgaged to the hilt and falling down about the hero's ears, his spendthrift brother is in hiding from clamoring creditors, his aged mother has nightmares about ending her life in the poorhouse, his sisters dream futilely of proper come-outs even as they resign themselves to the necessity of becoming governess' or paid companions, and the hero himself is staring at a mountain of gambling debts that in all honor must be paid before the butcher's bill.

This hero feels insecure about the future and trapped by circumstances. He is weighted down by responsibilities. He cannot join his peers in their expensive entertainments. His dire financial straits are known or suspected by society and he is looked upon as a fortune-hunter. As a consequence, wealthy and noble houses warn their daughters against him and if he cannot win one of these young ladies despite her parents' opposition, then he must look to the trades for his bride.

The wealthy and nobly born heroine is exceedingly fortunate. She is cosseted, her every whim is seen to, and she is able to indulge herself however she pleases within the bounds of propriety. She has no need to think of the future and she accepts as a matter of course the admiration and flattery bestowed upon her. Her destiny is one of idle luxury as the wife of an equally wealthy and noble gentleman. It never occurs to her to wonder what life would be like as a governess or a paid companion.

The poor but nobly born heroine is in much the same straits as her counterpart, the poor but nobly born hero. However, whereas it is his responsibility to marry well, it is her duty to do so. She must accept the best possible offer, no matter what her feelings about the gentleman, in order to save her family from financial ruin, to spare her parents the further expense of her upkeep, and to make possible a brighter future for her siblings.

The wealthy heroine of merely respectable birth, such as the daughter of a trades merchant, is situated a bit better than the poor but nobly born heroine. She has the opportunity of "marrying up" and aligning her family with a noble line. Though she herself may never be completely comfortable or accepted in the exalted society that she becomes a.part of, her descendents will be members of the aristocracy.

The poor heroine who is of merely respectable birth has the most difficult role. She hopes to better her situation in the world, but reality grants her few options in earning her way. These options include the positions of governess and paid companion; a gentleman's mistress; and an actress dancer (which almost invariably meant becoming someone's mistress, as well). Other possibilities were to go into service as a lady's maid, a housemaid, a cook, or a scullery maid; or to go into the employ of a modiste or milliner.

Her father is probably a country squire, a vicar, a soldier or sailor, or a tradesman. Each of these types of parent will somehow have been able to provide the genteel polish required of the heroine, whether through the offices of a well-bred mother or other female relation who has raised the girl or through an exacting finishing school. It is paramount that this heroine be well-bred in manner and thought if she is to be able to fit into high society once she has caught the hero's attention.

At first glance, this heroine's opportunities for dazzling matrimonial offers are not broad. She has little access to high society and thus she cannot really hope to catch the eye of a wealthy noble. The poor but nobly born gentleman cannot afford to consider her, even if he was to become aware of her existence. Again, she runs in quite different circles of society. Her choices realistically consist of the neighboring squire's son, the vicar, the soldier or sailor, the tradesman's son, the innkeeper or the stolid yeoman. Since the hero of the regency romance must be noble, it is "fate" that must bring this particular heroine to the hero's notice.

We now have two distinctive types of hero and four types of heroine. Depending upon the attributes assigned to the hero and the heroine, and the circumstances thrust upon them, each combination and choice automatically brings along an attached set of consequences. These consequences, or conflicts, are what will drive the developments of relationship and, in the final analysis, of plot.

When the characters are thrown into situations that, for them, are as unfamiliar as possible, great character conflict will result. Certainly, this conflict relies heavily on their opposite character's circumstances and personality.

The wealthy and nobly born hero can choose any of the four heroines. If is he arrogant, cynical and hard-hearted, there is nothing in his life to challenge him or stimulate his intellectual capabilities or even to threaten his emotions. This becomes the heroine's job.

If the wealthy and nobly born hero is proud and bored, and perhaps possessing a heart well-guarded because of a previous hurtful experience, the heroine's job is to renew his faith in love and to earn his trust.

The poor but nobly born hero can choose all but the poor heroine of merely respectable birth. The resolution of the hero's financial problems are a major factor in the story. The heroine's job is naturally to provide the means for the hero to overcome his financial difficulties, but she also must convince him that he is not a lesser man for being forced to accept her help.

The wealthy and nobly born heroine can choose either hero. This heroine may be proud, bored and sophisticated. She would like to find someone, but the gentlemen she knows are too much like herself to be interesting. The hardened and cynical hero must have an utterly incredible personality to engage her interest. In fact, if this hero is determined to have her, he must force her to take serious notice of him.

This heroine is more likely to be drawn to the wealthy and nobly born hero who keeps such guard over his once-vulnerable heart, or to the poor but nobly born hero, whose pride is battered but yet he survives with dignity.

The poor but nobly born heroine must choose the wealthy and nobly born hero. This heroine is a character of kindness, pride, strength, and dignity. The cold arrogant gentleman with the hard heart initially considers her a necessary inconvenience or simply an object of lust, but he is eventually won over by her sterling character. The gentleman whose heart is more vulnerable than he wants to admit accepts her presence into his life in a kinder manner, but he is perhaps harder to convince of the sincerity of her love.

The wealthy heroine of merely respectable birth can choose either the wealthy and nobly born hero or the poor but nobly born hero. This heroine is warm, kind and strong. She must be, in order to overcome the disadvantages of her birth in the eyes of society. She is well aware that she is "marrying up" and she doesn't have any false pride about herself. This humble quality, matched with her other character attributes, is a potent combination that eventually gains her the respect and love of whichever hero she plays opposite of.

The poor heroine of merely respectable birth can only choose the wealthy and nobly born hero. This heroine has a firm grasp on reality. Relationships are not casual. Frivolity is unknown to her. Everything that she holds essential for her survival runs counter to the lifestyle of the wealthy and nobly born hero. She views his overtures with mistrust, suspects him of toying with her, and that he is only momentarily entertained by her. She asks herself what will happen to her when he wanders back out of her life.

If for some reason she marries the hero early in the book, she feels insecure and she waits for disaster to strike. She is afraid to love the hero, and when she does fall in love with him she despairs of ever attaining a happy ending. The hero's job is to earn her trust and her love. Perhaps he must first change his own selfish, hard-hearted and cynical nature before he is able to accomplish this purpose. Or perhaps he must realize that his own deeply-buried vulnerability is the key to freeing the heroine of her insecurity. Whatever the particular case, the differences in attributes between these two characters are fraught with tension and missteps that inevitably create conflict.

A good rule of thumb to keep the conflict between characters ongoing and sizzling is to remember that every scene in the book must have a point. There must be something tangible that can be derived. This might be a leap in romantic tension, or the growing dislike of one character for another, or the unease that a character might feel about an upcoming event. Irregardless, every scene must do its job of carrying forward the story just that little bit more. Otherwise, the conflict between the characters loses momentum and becomes stilted, a result that is swiftly followed by the reader's cracking yawn.

The point of each scene is attained through the use of unfamiliar situations, to which the characters must react, and the characters' personality differences. Certainly many of these scenes will be thought out in advance during the plotting stage of the book, but often new scenes or situations arise during the actual writing that do not seem to have a particular point. I find it extremely helpful to decide just what I want to accomplish by the scene, which is the furthering of character relationships or plot or both. This helps me to focus in on the basic thread of the story.

Some scenes are much easier to focus in on than others. Romantic scenes and physical action scenes are very similar in that both are fast-paced and both showcase character conflict. These types of scenes are much easier to write than other, calmer, scenes because the point of the scene is a readily apparent quantity.

For example, in a romantic scene, the heroine and the hero discover exciting and erotic fireworks blazing to life between them. However, the heroine is not yet ready to admit to the hero that she is in love with him. She fights her own feelings as well as his perception of those same feelings. This conflict is the point of the scene. It nicely wraps up the eroticism into a package that deepens the stakes of the relationship between the heroine and the hero. This in turn will generate future evolutions in their relationship. The hero can later recall, for instance, how the heroine responded to his lovemaking before she turned back into the prim and proper miss once more. He will wonder whether it was his over-active imagination, or he might decide that the heroine is not as indifferent as she pretends. In either case, he will undoubtedly want to satisfy his own curiosity concerning the heroine's feelings. This ambition will naturally be stiff-armed or otherwise, and cleverly, avoided by the wary heroine. *Viola*, the groundwork for more character conflict has been laid.

The use of the romantic scene will naturally be pivotal in a romance. The scene should be placed so that it is central to the ongoing story and advances the plot. Also, the scene by its very nature has a high degree of tension. The characters involved in the romantic scene somehow reveal more of themselves and their personalities. All of these requirements are indicated in the example given above. What is not illustrated is the kind of language used in a romantic scene. Language is a very individual thing for a writer. There are a hundred ways to convey a passionate moment between characters, but do keep in mind that rich and evocative language goes further in creating the spirit of true hearts-and-butterflies romance than does pornographic, clinical, cliched, or even overmodest language.

In a physical action scene, the point is generally far different from that of a romantic scene. However, again the result is an easy quantity to assess. When a duel takes place between the hero and the villain, one or the other could be wounded. Which one is chosen to sport the interesting bandages depends upon what is supposed to happen later in the plot. The character conflict is probably a combination of the verbal duelling and the actual physical action of shooting at one another, with all the strong attendant feelings of anger, hatred, fear, or resignation. The point of the scene is mainly to further the plot.

Compare the two foregoing examples to an ordinary ballroom scene in which the heroine and the hero make polite conversation. The point of the scene is not as readily apparent, yet there must be something to come of this conversation in a social setting that will enhance the struggle in the relationship and that will move the plot along.

Perhaps the heroine does not dance well and as a consequence she has decided to limit herself to country dances only, which are not as likely to point up her deficiencies. The hero requests that she dance a waltz with him.

She makes a smiling excuse. He just as agreeably insists. The heroine naturally begins to feel that she is being forced into a position of either acquiescing or of creating a scene in front of a roomful of witnesses. She acquiesces and the hero is granted his dance; but at what cost? This, then, becomes the point of a very ordinary scene. Perhaps nothing too terribly important has been said between the heroine and the hero; yet their conversation has conveyed conflict and the subsequent consequences of the hero's insistence are yet to be reckoned. In addition, the reader has been given a bit of insight into the two characters themselves and will subsequently begin to expect a certain type of reaction from these characters when they are faced with similar circumstances.

Character conflict is nothing more than bringing together characters who hold conflicting views or beliefs, or characters who are situated so differently that their circumstances force a clashing of opinion and of will.

The best character conflict is created by threatening the character's self-image. Assign specific personality and circumstantial attributes to each character so that what the character thinks about himself or herself is readily apparent to the reader. Then thrust the character into situations and conversations that directly challenge the character to defend his or her self-image. This makes for ripping good reading. The reader will be captivated by the characters' struggle to reconcile their self-image with their own actions and changing thoughts.

The various attributes that can be used to create a character's self-image are described in the following chapters on the heroine, the hero, and secondary characters.

Chapter Four

THE HEROINE

The heroine and the hero of the regency romance are imbued with certain characteristics, or attributes. I have devoted a separate chapter to each character so that these attributes can be dealt with in detail.

The heroine is a spirited young woman. She is likely to act on her own or on someone else's behalf rather than sit back and helplessly wring her hands. She is also independent enough to offer some counterpoint of opinion to that of the hero or to some of the other characters. Or the heroine may be more meek in temperament rather than overtly independent; nevertheless, she has the moral courage to stand up for herself when the situation calls upon her to do so.

She is anywhere from seventeen years of age, when she is just leaving the schoolroom, to around twenty-six, at which great age the young lady who was still unmarried was considered to have been "on the shelf" for some years.

The heroine is occasionally older. In my own book, *The Waltzing Widow*, the heroine was a widow of thirty-four years of age, who had a son in Wellington's army and a seventeen year old daughter who was just being brought out into society. In the weeks leading up to and during the Battle of Waterloo, the widow found a second love in the person of a nobleman of comparable age and circumstances. I had originally intended for the heroine to be thirty-eight, but my editor deemed that too old for a romantic lead. However, the heroine could not have been any younger than thirty-four, otherwise the existence of her two grown children, upon whom relied much of the conflict in the plot, would have been impossible.

The heroine is intelligent and educated. Perhaps she is even reputed to be a "bluestocking", a reputation that was a horrible drawback to her matrimonial chances in the eyes of less cerebral gentlemen and to the matron whose responsibility it is to marry her off.

The heroine possesses the social graces. She can converse easily in a light, polite style. She dances well. She can sketch and watercolor. She can play an instrument with passable technical skill. She embroiders beautifully, speaks fluent French, and sets an elegant table. Most important of all, she has an innate unerring instinct for satisfying her gentleman's wishes. In short, the perfect regency heroine combines the role of today's corporate hostess with that of the consummate actress/artist.

Any and all of these requirements are made to be broken. After all, perfection in the heroine can be, and is, deadly boring. However, the heroine may indeed possess all of the above requirements and still be utterly human. For example, create a heroine who is reluctant to marry a particular gentleman. She may be older and has grown up in a house where she was given the order of the place. She runs the household, does the accounts, and listens to the complaints of the estate dependents. She is independent and perhaps lacking, or is rusty in, the social graces of polite conversation and submissive agreeableness. She likes herself as she is. Why should she marry, she asks. Why, indeed. The hero must offer something special to the heroine, and must himself be special to overlook the heroine's "flawed character".

The heroine is usually pretty, sometimes devastatingly beautiful. She may sometimes be only "pleasant of countenance" but possess redeeming qualities such as a shining abundance of hair, incredible eyes, or a striking kindness of manner.

Her fashion sense is impeccable. Her preferred style of dress is anything but frumpish. If she hasn't the money to spend on a fashionable wardrobe, she yet establishes about herself an air of neatness, of prettiness without fluffy frills, sensible and in good taste. There is nothing flashy or faddish about the heroine, unless she deliberately sets out to score a point against the hero.

The heroine is nearly always of respectable birth, but not necessarily a member of the peerage or from a wealthy family. These factors can be mixed for maximum impact depending on the story-line.

Wealthy and nobly born

> Poor but nobly born
> Wealthy but of merely respectable birth
> Poor and of merely respectable birth

As you can imagine, given that the heroine and the hero's romance is played out against the backdrop of high society, these combinations have a great deal to do with how the action and the misunderstandings that make up the plot are put together.

A wealthy and nobly born heroine is a prime catch in the gentleman's eyes. She brings wealth and a noble line to add to a gentleman's own antecedents.

A poor but nobly born heroine probably needs to marry so that her family will no longer suffer the financial burden of providing for her. She is still a good catch, depending upon how exalted her family name. In this case, the fortune-hunters won't have any interest in the heroine. It is gentlemen with social aspirations or those already wealthy enough not to care about the heroine's lack of dowry who will pursue her.

The wealthy heroine who is of merely respectable birth won't be looked at by gentlemen who are very proud of their family lineage. However, fortune-hunters will sniff about this heroine's heels with only slightly less enthusiasm than they do the wealthy and noble young lady. These latter gentlemen will also feel they have a better chance with this young lady, (better than they would with one more socially exalted), because their family name is probably more prominent than hers; her family will welcome a connection into the peerage. Another deciding factor in favor of this heroine from the fortune-hunters point of view is that their own lack of fortune will usually be a matter of record and naturally the wealthy and noble young lady's family will guard her against them.

The poor heroine who is of merely respectable birth is in dire straits. She cannot offer either proud family lineage or a substantial dowry to entice a gentleman. She can offer beauty, however, and if she is guarded ferociously by her family she might receive an eligible offer from a gentleman who doesn't care much about the lack of dowry and who isn't particularly determined to add illustrious ancestry to his descendents' bloodline. If this beauty has instead negligent or greedy relations who do not guard her virtue, then the proposals that the heroine will receive will not be of the marriage kind. She will be pressed to become some gentleman's mistress and discover to her dismay that her relations urge this less than respectable course on her, either because they mistakenly believe that the gentleman can be later shamed into marriage or simply because they want to get her off their hands as quickly as possible.

Now let's add the social graces or lack thereof to this stew.

The wealthy and nobly born heroine who is only passable in looks, or who is considered downright plain by unkind relations, can still be expected to get a man. However, her character must overcome her lack of conventional beauty. In addition, this heroine always somehow turns from the ugly duckling into a rare swan in the eyes of the hero.

The wealthy and nobly born heroine who is independent and very selective in her suitors, who is a bluestocking, who forthrightly and unerringly pinpoints the failings of her suitors, will inevitably put off some of the eligible gentlemen. Her character and her reputation will naturally create conflict with the hero.

Perhaps instead, the heroine is tone-deaf. She is also unable to paint well because she is clumsy with pen or brush and she is impossible on the dance-floor. Or, she is unbearably shy in company. The gentleman who can overlook these social flaws to discover her true character, and in the process aid her in overcoming her detriments, is definitely her hero.

A summary of the possible social attributes to assign the heroine includes the following.
1) Good family, or less desirable relations;
2) Gracious manners, or abrupt and decided style;
3) Wealth, or lack of;
4) Ability to play hostess;
5) Ability to handle a household and servants;
6) Personal talents, such as singing, proficiency in an instrument, dancing, painting, flower arranging, needlework, fluency in French.

The regency heroine's other areas of attributes can also be summarized. Please keep in mind that for every positive attribute, there is also one considered less desirable in the "perfect" regency lady. By mixing up the possibilities between the positive and the less desirable attributes, the heroine becomes uniquely individual. This is what makes creating characters fun.

Physical attributes
1) Short, medium height, tall;
2) Slender, plump, willowy, lithe, athletic, statuesque;

3) Hair is blonde, brunette, red, black; heavy, abundant, fine; curling, straight;
4) Eyes are large, expressive; gentle, myopic, sparkling; black, brown, gray, hazel, blue, green, amber;
5) Features are dazzlingly beautiful, pleasant, impish, regular;
6) Figure is big-bosomed, small bosomed; outrageously curved; nicely curved, appealingly curved.

Though it is a temptation to make the heroine a veritable goddess, surely it is more realistic for any given female to be little more than pretty. Heroines of regency romances tend to be very attractive, but they are rarely devastatingly beautiful. For those who are beautiful, their beauty is often used as a source of misunderstanding and conflict. As an example, a renowned beauty may find that she is denied the pleasure of simply talking to a gentleman; rather, the gentleman is always an admirer who is more interested in paying her fulsome compliments or finagling a moonlit kiss. This heroine would be instantly drawn to a hero who pays not the least heed to her beauty. She will be piqued and even insulted by his apparent indifference, but at the same time she will take particular note of him.

Character attributes
    1) Independent;
    2) Stubborn;
    3) Gracious;
    4) Kind;
    5) Patient;
    6) Social conscience, i.e., an interest in social reform;
    7) Tact, or occasional lack of;
    8) Well-read, capable of reasoning and logic;
    9) Insecure for one reason or another;
    10) Hasty, or even, temper;
    11) Strength of will, i.e., lack of interest in the opinion of others; belief in herself and her ideals.

Most regency heroines tend to possess an inordinate degree of independence, which in reality is probably more characteristic of our modern society than it was of the regency era. The social structure during the Regency was more rigid and did not allow the same latitude that women enjoy today. Nevertheless, the regency heroine is imbued with this attribute and she is well-liked by the readers for it.

Emotional attributes
1) Need for security, love, companionship, and sincerity;
2) Hope for all of the above;
3) Fears the disillusionment of the above; also, possible fears could include claustrophobia, shyness in company, fear of water, horses, etc.

Some may be surprised that a romance character is given such a detailed dossier that it might even include a fear of horses, such as was possessed by my heroine in *Lord John's Lady*. However, that is just the sort of thing that makes the character seem more appealing and more real to the reader. In addition, these quirky little fears can be used as plot devices. In *A Chance Encounter,* the heroine was allergic to roses and her allergy played a small role in partially resolving a particular character conflict.

The regency heroine's primary concern is romance. Either she is actively looking or hoping for an object of romance, or she resists the idea of marriage altogether. In the first instance, she must snare the hero's interest; in the second, the hero must capture her heart.

Everything is secondary to the evolving romance. The plot might involve a bit of mystery for the heroine to solve or a touch of slapstick when she must resolve another character's romantic entanglement, but these subplots are simply smaller mirrors for the main thread of the story - the romance. However, the heroine's character makeup and her emotional state at various stages in the story - such as her suspicions of the hero during the unwinding of the mystery or her disbelief of the other character's propensity for trouble - all contribute to and influence the progress to a satisfying denouement of the romance.

Any of the factors mentioned can be mixed and matched to create points of conflict and unique situations for the heroine. Some of the conflict may even be staged solely within the heroine's own turbulent thoughts, as when her heart tells her one thing about the hero even as her mind is cautioning her against him.

The point of view from which the story is told is mainly that of the heroine. Since most romance readers are women, it stands to reason that this audience will empathize most strongly with a female point of view. Therefore, the heroine's thoughts, feelings, and opinions shape much of the resulting direction of the book. At a guess, I'd say that 60% to 70% of the book is told through the heroine's eyes.

This does not mean that the hero is merely standing around hoping that his side will be adequately told through the heroine's perceptions. Far from it. In today's romances, the hero is no longer the silent enigma. The reader is also made privy to his thoughts and feelings, though often not to the same extent as those of the heroine.

Other characters also let the reader inside their heads, but far less often than either the heroine or the hero. Generally, when the point of view is briefly lent to secondary characters, it is because their thoughts shed direct insight on how the heroine or the hero are reacting to the situation at hand. For example, the hero's friend might reflect worriedly that he has never before seen the hero appear so distraught over a woman's caprice. He realizes suddenly that the hero must actually be in love for the first time. The friend might also feel a sense of foreboding over what the hero might feel compelled to do next. In a matter of three lines, three things have been accomplished: 1) The reader is shown the hero without using the old technique of having the character look into a mirror and himself catalog his distraught appearance; 2) The reader is told that it is highly likely that the hero is in love with the heroine, but that he is not finding it a particularly salubrious experience; and, 3) The reader is told that the hero is probably going to react in a wild and illogical way to this new experience.

It is confusing, not to mention damaging, to the consistency of the story to flip-flop the viewpoint from character to character. It interrupts the flow of the story and it also disrupts the gathering empathy that is building in the reader's mind for the character through whose perceptions the scene is being told. I try to write each chapter, or each scene, mainly from one character's viewpoint. If the viewpoint must change to get the whole and desired effect out of the scene, then each character's viewpoint is encapsulated in separate paragraphs. It is not a good idea to juxtapose the heroine's viewpoint next to that of the hero, or any other character, within the same paragraph. If you do, the scene reads like a rapid exchange on the tennis court. By separating changes in viewpoint at least by paragraph, the reader's empathy for the characters will remain undisturbed.

One particular factor that I have not touched on yet at any length is social reform. The regency period carried the seeds of what would become the age of social reform: orphanages, public education, hospital care, prevention of cruelty to children and animals, child-labor laws, aid to the poor, etc. These matters were considered radical, even dangerous, but they were discussed. Though the main thrust of the social reform movement had its roots in the developing middle class, some of the aristocracy were becoming interested.

Arm in arm with these ideas marched the evangelical movement. Religion was an integral part of these people's lives, to one extent or another.

Whether a character is a sincere churchgoer or attends merely as a matter of form - this is a question that should be posed on the behalf of the fictional characters because so much of the social life was intimately tied to the church. Does the heroine embroider beautiful altar cloths for her local parish church or arrange flowers for the Sunday service? Is the hero so completely cynical that he feels contempt for anyone who confesses to the milder gifts of mercy and compassion? Will the heroine and the hero be married by special license or will there be a grand society wedding at St. George's Cathedral? Does the hero feel compelled to provide financial support for a newly founded orphanage?

If done with a light touch, so that the romance is not overshadowed by other such serious matters as social reform and religious beliefs, the heroine or the hero or both can have an abiding and enlightened interest in these things. However, any such interest will usually call for a change in setting, such as scenes placed in the poorer part of London or a descriptive discussion of the waifs huddled in a county poorhouse. This naturally detracts from the glittering backdrop of aristocratic society which is one of the mainstays of the regency romance. Again, the primary thread - the romance - cannot be lost or the book becomes something quite other than a regency romance.

This is not to say that serious matters should not be touched upon. These areas of interest can be used to great effect to create a touch of tension or to generate conflict, or even humor, in the story. Anything that has a human-interest angle is most effective in capturing reader attention. Fictional characters who dare to take strong stands on controversial social and religious issues are made that much more flesh-and-blood. Just remember that the heroine's primary concern is romance and place everything else into the perspective of providing interesting sidelights into character or of providing subplots.

The heroine practices leisurely pursuits, such as those listed under the social attributes. However, more physical interests may include fox hunting, coursing hares, archery, marksmanship, fencing (unusual), sailing or punting, coaching or driving, and falconry. She may also study herbs, gardening or agriculture, and the proper breeding of horses and hounds. (The last mentioned might coincide nicely with the search for a suitable mate possessing his own impressive lineage, as any maiden aunt with a passion for genealogy would inform the heroine.)

The regency heroine can be as active or leisure-loving as you wish. Society as a whole was restrictive, yes. Tradition was restrictive, true. But balance against these restrictions the British love of animals and hunting, as well as the tenor of times that encompassed war, social unrest and reform, and the industrial revolution, and you will discover that there is room for the regency heroine to express herself.

Thus far, we have talked about the heroine who is situated as the daughter of the house. We can place the heroine in other circumstances as well, though always keeping in mind that she must somehow fit within the mold of the foregoing four types of heroine.

The heroine can be in a position of employment, perhaps as a governess or a paid companion. Obviously these heroines would fit into the poor but nobly born or the poor but of respectable birth categories.

The heroine who takes the position of governess to the children of a brooding hero has been done many, many times; beware that you do not fall into the trap of plowing old ground. Give it a new twist. Perhaps the heroine becomes governess to the hero's younger brothers and sisters. In this situation, the hero can be the careless-seeming scion of the house. Or perhaps the hero's father and young step-mother die unexpectedly in a carriage accident, leaving him responsible for his half-siblings. This hero won't be quite as carefree as the scion but he need not be brooding, either; actually, he is probably harassed out of his mind trying to deal with the children.

The heroine could also be a poor relation whose position is not a particularly happy one. She relies on the charity of sometimes insensitive relations and she may be expected to show her gratitude for being taken in by taking on the role of all-around gopher. Again, this situation has been done before. It must be handled carefully if it is not to seem old-hat to the reader. A twist on the old theme might be that, instead of playing a Cinderella role, the heroine becomes the much-cosseted and beloved adopted daughter of the childless couple that took her in. Complications may possibly arise through her parents' suddenly reduced circumstances, or through the appearance of a hero who is honor-bound to provide for the heroine upon her parents' death. Perhaps the hero pays court to the heroine because he wishes to ally himself with her parents' family, and even though she is adopted, she is still their beloved daughter. Regardless, it would be an interesting challenge to portray this heroine as other than the abused poor relation.

Rarely seen but certainly rife with possibilities would be a heroine who qualifies as a spinster. She would naturally not be too terribly old, at most in her early thirties, but old enough that her relations have long since given up any expectation of her marrying. She can be a maiden aunt or the willful daughter of the house. She either has an independence of her own or she is dependent on the largesse of some one of her relations. She acts as hostess for an unmarried brother or she takes on the role of the family's extra hand at whatever task needs doing, handling the mundane and the crisis alike with competence and patience. She can eschew men as rather foolish creatures, never having met one who touched her heart, or she was in love once and for one reason or another the romance did not come off happily.

The regency heroine can also be a young widow, with even a small child to provide for. The child may play an excellent minor secondary role, but must never be allowed to detract from the development of the romance between the heroine and the hero. In my second book, *The Demon Rake*, the heroine had a young daughter for whom she wanted to provide. However, neither the heroine's late husband's family, the members of which she had never met because her husband had been estranged from them, nor the reader knew of the child until the hero guessed the fact of the girl's existence.

I was able, then, to establish a relationship between the heroine and the hero before the child ever appeared on stage. This tactic breathed a touch of mystery into the heroine's otherwise straight-forward character - a dichotomy that eventually puzzled the hero so much that he began questioning his own rashly formed assumptions about the heroine.

The widowed heroine is naturally concerned to find a good father for her child. This factor will be a prime influence on who and why she chooses her next mate. However, her own attachment to the gentleman must be primary. There may be a decent fellow who would make a splendid stepfather, but who does not make the heroine's heart sing or her breath catch when she is with him. This worthy is therefore and most definitely not the hero.

The true hero is yet to be introduced.

Chapter Five

THE HERO

The regency hero can be as straightforward or as complex as you like. He is always a member of the aristocracy, though not necessarily a peer. In other words, he can be a younger son or an heir presumptive (the nephew or cousin of a duke, etc. who will inherit in the event of no direct male heirs).

The hero is usually wealthy, but sometimes not. He is either incredibly handsome or rather interestedly craggy in appearance. His attire is perfection or fashionably negligent. He is the byword of suavity or is known for his careless, even rude, manners.

At this point, I'd like to add a special observation. Among the aristocracy, the paler one's skin the better. The reason was that sun-browned skin marked someone as a laborer - as someone who worked for his living (horrors!).

When we write of the heroine who is somewhat tanned of face, it is because she spends a lot of time on horseback, hunting, walking about her father's estate, etc., and she has neglected to wear a protective hat or to carry with her at all times a parasol. This neglect of one's skin was disapproved of by starchy matrons and frowned upon by gentlemen who were very conscious of other's opinions.

Similarly, a hero who possesses a tan should indicate that he also tramps about the fields or spends much of his waking hours hunting. It also is characteristic of a soldier, who necessarily must spend his life outdoors, or of a gentleman who has spent a few to several years out in India.

Today, our ideal is the suntanned healthy look. But during most of history, a tan often and instantly placed the possessor outside the aristocracy. Writers tend to overlook this one area of historical difference when describing their heros, who are invariably nicely sun-browned.

Today's readers are probably not too keen on having a lily-white hero, since for us a tan instantly connotes health and good looks. However, there is nothing to say that a lily-white hero might not work very well, given other characteristics that provoke enough interest in him to overcome the reader's instant aversion to what seems an unhealthy drawback.

The hero is intelligent, either overtly described as so or the fact emerges through the action of the story rather than through physical description. A placid, patient gentleman might give the impression of fewer brains to some of the other characters who do not know him well, until his mettle is tested in some manner that proves beyond a shadow of doubt that he is very intelligent, indeed.

The hero must appeal to the feminine heart. He is usually either the type who is dangerous and needs the taming of an all-encompassing love to bring out his best qualities, or he is the type who appears from the outset to be a gentleman who will provide security and a serene relationship once his heart is captured.

It is much easier to write about a hero who has one or more negative character attributes that he must overcome than it is to write about a hero who is an all-around nice fellow. For example, the hero may be arrogant, cynical, and possess a smouldering temper. This combination lends itself well to conflict with the other characters. The heroine will naturally resent the hero's arrogance; she will defend herself against the hero's cynical view of women in general and, in particular, his cynicism regarding her own motives; she will constantly provoke the hero's temper, whether intentionally or not.

On the other hand, the hero who is mild of temperament, who has not allowed his exalted social position go to his head, and who is likeable rather than dangerous is more difficult to manipulate into situations of conflict. The heroine feels immediate trust in this hero and she thinks of him as a friendly sort with whom she is both comfortable and safe.

This hero's personality is more subtle than the other. At first glance he is not the fascinating and sexually dangerous gentleman that will most appeal to the reader. However, by choosing with extra care this hero's other emotional and character attributes, a most popular hero can be created.

In order to make this metamorphosis, the likeable hero needs a pronounced fatal flaw in order for sparks to be set flying between himself and the heroine. He could be extremely protective of the heroine, for instance. He sees villains everywhere and as a consequence he is always butting in when he is least wanted. Perhaps the heroine is delighting in a light flirtation with another gentleman. She will hardly be put in a grateful mood when the over-protective hero suddenly appears to whisk her away, and on the flimsiest of excuses, too. The heroine will react with frustration and anger.

This preliminary conflict can be the basis of a humorous sequence of events that escalates the conflict between the heroine and the hero to such a height that the hero is actually in danger of losing the lady that he loves. When the hero realizes that he is on the verge of permanently destroying any chance of a relationship with the heroine, he will force back his protective instincts and give her breathing room. Naturally, this occurs just when a real villain has real designs on the heroine. The hero can then step in and show the stuff he is made of.

The gentleman must also possess social attributes, and two sets of them to boot. The hero must naturally be able to relate to his peers. He must have an interest, whether keen or passing, in "manly" sports. This includes, but is not restricted to, hunting of all sorts, racing, pugilistics, gambling, marksmanship, duelling and fencing. He is educated and may have an interest in antiquities, social reform, agriculture, industry and machinery, finances (as in loaning and investing and trading), the arts, the breeding of horses and hounds, and the collecting of snuffs.

The hero should also possess certain qualities acceptable to the ladies. He possesses an elegant "leg", or bow. He has the ability to make charming conversation or to flirt with outrageous wit. He is at least a passable dancer. He must have a willingness to "do the proper", as in fulfilling the role of an extra gentleman at a ball or supper by devoting himself to escorting or dancing with the unescorted ladies young and old.

Naturally, if the hero is rude and negligent of fashionable opinion, a brooding rake, or otherwise a social scapegrace, he has redeeming qualities that still make of him a sought-after guest. He has looks and is of excellent family. He's wealthy and perhaps has political ambition and contacts.

The hero is generally between the early twenties and the early thirties in age, with all the differences of temperament and circumstances that a decade may make in a gentleman's life. For instance, an older gentleman who has never married may have suffered a disillusioning love affair in his younger years, and is now wary of the snares thrown out by ambitious young ladies and their mothers. Or, as a young gentleman, he may be more impulsive or hasty-tempered than a man who has entered into his thirties. A young gentleman may not as yet have come into his full inheritance, or have learned the lesson that unstinting gambling and carousing can waste that same inheritance very quickly so that it becomes necessary for him to marry for money.

The hero has had a succession of tutors, he has likely gone to Cambridge or Oxford, and he has perhaps taken a Grand Tour of Europe (not as likely as in former times since the French Revolution and Napoleon's advent upon the Continent). In lieu of the customary Grand Tour, he has possibly been to the Greek Isles, to Egypt, the Middle East, or perhaps even to Russia. He can read and write Latin and Greek and he speaks passable, if not fluent, French.

The hero can be a rake. He may keep a mistress, who naturally falls by the wayside as he becomes interested in the heroine. Indeed, he may wish to set the heroine up as his newest ladylove, depending upon her circumstances in life and his own attitudes.

The hero possibly may not dabble in light-skirts at all, or he does so rarely that he is still looked upon as a safe, respectable gentleman who will be an appropriate escort for even a young and inexperienced young lady. However, his feelings for that same particular sweet or incorrigible young lady may not be so avuncular or disinterested by the end of the book.

This is all background that the writer must establish about the hero, if only in her own mind, if he is to be three-dimensional. As you can see, nearly anything goes with the hero. Like the heroine, the gentleman's attributes can be mixed and matched to make for an interesting grab-bag of situations.

Again, the story is played out against the backdrop of high society. The romance is the main story-line, while everything else influences or pushes it in whatever directions seem logical.

There are basically two possible regency heros.

> Wealthy and nobly born;
> Poor but nobly born.

As you can see, there is far less latitude in combinations for the hero than for the heroine. The hero must be nobly born. That is pretty much a basic given. He cannot be of merely respectable birth because then he has no legitimate access to the high society against which the story takes place. Unless he is for some reason raised to the peerage, more rare by the regency era, he must already be a member of the aristocracy. (A gentleman was raised to the peerage in cases of extreme service to king and country, such as in the case of the Duke of Wellington, who rose from the position of younger son and ended with a higher title than his elder brother, who had succeeded to their father's title. The duke was, however, an extraordinarily able general who ultimately saved England and all of Europe from conquest by that other military genius, Napoleon Bonaparte.)

A wealthy and nobly born hero is the ultimate catch in the eyes of the aristocratic matrons with marriageable daughters. He combines impeccable lineage with worldly comforts and excesses.

This hero is usually pressured to take a wife who matches him in background and lineage and wealth. Often, though, he stubbornly pursues someone less desirable and sometimes quite ineligible by the standards set by society. This hero in the throes of love cares nothing about dowry and little about proper lineage. Even if the young lady has tradespeople for relations, he can overlook it, especially if the relations recognize and keep to their own place. If the relations prove to be intrusively vulgar or greedy, he can be quite ruthless in forcing his wishes upon them. This hero, depending upon his character attributes, is also the most likely to want to make a beguiling beauty into his mistress rather than his wife.

The hero can be the younger son, still wealthy, but not of such high social prominence as his brother, the heir. However, he has established a firm position for himself among a circle of friends and acquaintances and he is generally sought after by hostesses in need of an extra gentleman.

The poor but nobly born hero is in a difficult position. He must marry wealth to keep his family name afloat, and preferably a young lady of equally noble birth. However, opportunity often dictates reality and this hero must settle for a lady from a wealthy but merely respectable family. He is often trapped in the guise of a fortune-hunter, which he detests but cannot easily shed. It is his strong character and sterling qualities that eventually convince heroine and reader alike that his pecuniary motives have always been tempered by nobleness of heart.

The poor but nobly born younger son is in even worse straits than his brother the heir. He is definitely a fortune-hunter, and he can make that fortune by contracting a brilliant yet unlikely marriage, or go off to India and eventually return a wealthy nabob who can command the bride of his choice. Or he can go soldiering in hopes of swift promotion during the course of the war. He usually marries a young lady of respectable birth with a "genteel" dowry or one of noble birth who has the misfortune to be one of several daughters and who does not stand out in any degree either in looks or accomplishments or in the portion settled upon her.

This gentleman, the poor but nobly born younger son, often works quite well as a strong secondary character, providing a foil for his brother who is the actual hero.

The hero can be a widower and even have a small child. One of his considerations in finding a wife is to provide a good mother for his child, but the child can never be allowed to overshadow the romance that is developing between the hero and the heroine.

The hero's attributes can be divided into four major groupings: physical, social, character, and emotional. The choice of attributes plays a great part in determining how the hero acts and reacts to the heroine or to the circumstances that affect them both.

Physical attributes:
  1) height - short, medium height, tall, extremely tall;
  2) build - stock, slender, lithe, athletic, trim;
  3) hair - blond, brunette, red, black;
  4) eyes - color, size keenness, brilliance;
  5) movement - lazy, indolent, alert, lithe, studied, nervous energy;
  6) countenance - handsome, craggy, hawkish, browned, pale, sleepy, dissolute, hard, smiling, pleasant;
  7) presence - menacing, comfortable, riveting.

Obviously, the hero who gives off a menacing aura is more likely to be a cynical man, a hard-hearted man, a man who enjoys the sexual chase. This hero probably lets the heroine know very quickly that neither she nor any other woman means very much to him. He often seems menacing because he makes it quite clear that his intentions are not at all honorable and the object of his determined pursuit is to make the heroine into his mistress. The menacing hero could also be one who uses anger, cynicism, etc., to hide and protect a once-devastated heart.

This hero can be tall and large, but often actual physical size has little to do with a man's presence. Napoleon Bonaparte was a short man and yet he was so charismatic that he was able to come back from ignoble exile and raise an army that required the combined powers of Europe and Russia to defeat.

The hero's presence is not as potent on such a grand scale as this. However, when he walks into a room of people, whether he can be described as menacing or not, there should be something about him that commands attention - his personality, the way he carries himself, sheer physical size, whatever.

Something should be said, too, about physical handicaps. During the Regency, England was involved in two wars. The War of 1812 was fought against the former colonies in the Americas; the Napoleonic War was fought from 1803 to 1815 on the European continent. It was certainly not unheard-of to encounter gentlemen in London society who had suffered physical losses, such as of an arm or a leg. Very rarely, however, will the regency romance hero be one of these gentlemen.

Once again, Georgette Heyer must be given credit for establishing a precedent. By the end of *The Infamous Army*, the hero, who performed his military duties gallantly during the Battle of Waterloo, has suffered amputation of a shattered forearm. Does the heroine turn from him in disgust or fear? Not on your life. Neither does the reader. The tempestuous romance between these two characters is so strongly developed that the loss of an arm but emphasizes the poignancy of their feelings for one another.

In *Hearts Betrayed*, the hero had originally lost one arm at Waterloo. His handicap was essential to explain the perfectly horrible state of the relationship between the heroine and the hero. Before the book opens, the characters had once been engaged but had been torn apart by the war. The heroine thought the hero had died and he had allowed her to think so because he believed that she, after learning that he was wounded, had refused to have anything further to do with him. My editor hated the idea of a one-armed hero. So I gave the hero back his arm, but made clear that it did not work as well as it had before he was wounded. The story still worked wonderfully well. This was a compromise based on the editor's opinion of the marketplace.

Social attributes:
1) good family, whether heir or younger son;
2) gracious or elegant manners, or rude and abrupt style;
3) wealth, or lack of;
4) ability to handle household and servants;
5) ability to hold his own in "manly" pursuits/sports;
6) acceptable interests - arts, antiquities, agriculture, breeding of horses and hounds;
7) personal talents - dancing, elegant or flirtatious conversation, singing (at Christmas or while drinking with friends);
8) fashionable dress, whether perfect or negligent;
9) ability to play host.

The regency hero is rarely, if ever, employed. Trade and banking were occupations considered to be below an aristocrat. He might dabble in either as a hobby or as an investor, but his income never derives from such common pursuits. This is also true of the "gentleman farmer". He experiments with crops and breeding, new machines and drainage theories, but he is not dependent on his acreage for his very livelihood.

The aristocracy had open to them only three acceptable avenues of employment, and the gentlemen who pursued them were often younger sons who needed to establish their own place in the world because they could not rely upon an inheritance. The three honorable occupations were the military (including the navy), the diplomatic service, and the taking of orders (which meant entering the church, with usually the ambition to rise to a bishopric). I have read about Regency heros who were in either the military or the diplomatic service, but I have never encountered a story about one situated in orders.

<u>Character attributes</u>:
1) independence;
2) obstinateness;
3) ease of speaking feelings, or not;
4) hasty, or even, temper;
5) aggressive nature;
6) strength - physical or character, i.e., lack of interest in other's opinions;
7) well-read and educated;
8) social conscience (i.e., social reform; whether he takes a mistress or not);
9) patience or impatience;
10) arrogance;
11) kindness;
12) tact, or lack of on occasion;
13) well-hidden insecurity of one kind or another;
14) responsible (i.e., for family, reputation, honor);
15) honorable.

As I mentioned before, the hero who is quick to anger or who possesses any of the other more negative character attributes is easier to write about than the "perfect" gentleman. For some reason, we like to read about the hero that is unpredictable and wild and difficult to get along with - but, honestly, who would want to actually live with such a man? I doubt that very many of us would choose that particular man ahead of a gentleman who is unfailingly kind and patient and loving.

However, because that wonderful gentleman is more difficult to bring to life in the short scope of a romance, we rarely encounter him as the typical hero. Another reason, of course, is that in a romance it is often more exciting to have a demonstrable "Bad Boy" as the hero than the seemingly "Dull Joe". Just as readers have difficulty empathesizing with a perfect heroine, they can also manage little interest for the perfect gentleman. It would be difficult, indeed, to live up to the perfect man and his stringent standards and few of us care to think of ourselves in such a situation. That reader reluctance to accept a hero who is morally superior to the heroine pretty well destroys the believability of the romance before ever it takes off.

However, if the perfect gentleman is not quite so perfect as he initially appears, then this hero will surprise the readers. And he will thus have devastating appeal.

For the perfect hero to command the reader enthusiasm due him, he must possess some deficit in character, one that sets him into direct conflict with the heroine. If he is unfailingly kind, patient, and loving, this deficit will probably take the form of a negative emotional attribute.

Emotional attributes:
1) needs attention, sincerity, love, companionship;
2) fears vulnerability, loneliness; various possible phobias
   (water, climbing, sailing, horse-jumping,whatever);
   inattention, insincerity; lack of, or disillusionment in,
   love; ridicule, loss of face, dishonor;
3) hopes for "a decent life"; also, he hopes above needs
   will be met.

If the perfect hero is to sustain reader interest, he must possess emotional attributes that render him particularly vulnerable. Perhaps he is utterly incapable of expressing his innermost feelings and thus he is a misunderstood and lonely individual. The situation might be that the hero is blamed by others for something that happened in the past and he has never been able to articulate a proper defense that counters suspicion because to do so will expose his own fears. The heroine can at once sense the hero's loneliness, and even his need for her, but she discovers that she must struggle to persuade him to admit to his fears and to his vulnerability. Until the hero passes this monstrous hurdle, he will be incapable of expressing his love for the heroine. It goes without saying that the perfect hero probably uses his so-called perfections - courtesy, kindness, etc. - as shields so that the essential core of his being is deeply guarded against both discovery and possibly callous misunderstanding.

The regency hero's primary interest may not start out to be romance. He is not looking to begin with for a wife, or he is simply looking for a mistress. Or he is looking for a marriage of convenience that will insure his own and his family's future financial position.

The gentleman's character make-up, his emotional state, his social and physical attributes, all contribute to what happens to him during the course of the book. Generally, the hero is not in love to begin with. He must be persuaded, despite his own reservations, prejudices and obtuseness, that he is falling in love. Once that occurs, he must be willing to move heaven and earth to capture the heroine's heart and prove himself worthy of her. This should not be a simple task because it defines the conflict: the misunderstandings, and the circumstances, that constantly throw the hero and heroine together, only to tear them apart again. The progressions and setbacks in the romance act much like waves breaking on the beach, ebbing and flowing, until at last a calm pool catches and holds them fast.

Chapter Six

SECONDARY CHARACTERS

The secondary characters in a regency are very important. It is they who bring humor and villainy to the plot. The hero and heroine can't do without their leavening influence. Secondary characters serve the function of moving the plot along, many times skewing it into surprising directions. These characters can help along the romance between the heroine and the hero, or act to hinder it.

Secondary characters can take many guises, but more often than not they are close in relationship to either the heroine or the hero, or to both. Any close or extended family relation makes an excellent secondary character, such as a parent, aunt or uncle, brother or sister, or cousin.

The secondary character can be a friend or acquaintance to either the heroine or the hero, or is known to both. This character can be of either sex, though the heroine's friend is more likely to be a female and the hero's friend, a male, because it is more usual to have a close confidante of one's own sex. We tend to tell things to a friend of our own sex that we would never dream of mentioning to someone of the opposite sex simply because the latter cannot be expected to wholly understand our viewpoint, not having experienced it from the standpoint of gender.

The secondary characters that have been outlined are benign, friendly characters. There are also those who are less than devoted to the heroine and the hero's best interests, who might even wish one or the other, or both, ill-will. These are jealous relations, those who stand in succession if no marriage takes place, or whose envy of the heroine and the hero is due to their own insecurities. They are spurned suitors or mistresses. They are rivals for the heroine's or the hero's affections and they feel horribly threatened by the apparent success of another. They are obsessive or even evil.

A secondary (or even tertiary) character may also be an actual historical figure. The writer takes what is known about the historical figure's personality, mannerisms, views, and physical attributes to create a walk-on character, or even a strong secondary character that is essential to some element of the plot. Examples might be the Prince Regent, who was known to have liked pretty women about him; the Duke of Wellington, who was ever-cool on the battlefield; Beau Brummel, whose dictums on fashion could make or break a lady's or a gentleman's reputation for style; one of the patroness' of Almacks', who could withhold the coveted admission voucher that allowed a lady or a gentleman entry into that most exclusive of social clubs; Harriette Wilson, the famous *demimondaine* who competed with her sister for the gentlemen's favors. Whomever helps along the particular needs of your particular plot can be utilized. Remember only that these are historical personages and should not behave out of context of what is known about their lives.

Secondary character attributes can be divided into groupings similar to those of the heroine and the hero. These attributes are much more fluid for the secondary characters. They can literally be any combination under the sun to enable the writer to flesh out the action to which these characters are to contribute. However, their financial status, their lineage, and their physical attributes are not nearly as important as their other attributes.

Wealth, lineage and physical attributes do, of course, help to define the secondary characters, but closer attention should be paid to emotional, character, and social attributes. This is especially true in the case of a villainous character because motivation must be particularly strong. Emotional and character attributes are the factors that will matter most to the plot of the story, and predict how the characters' actions or reactions will affect the romance between the heroine and the hero.

Emotional attributes:
    1) needs attention, recognition (whether personal or social),
       love, security, reassurance, friendship;
    2) fears loneliness, ridicule, shame, humiliation;
       loss of face or honor; loss of inheritance;
       being left with the provision of an unwanted relation;

various phobias;
3) hopes for above needs for self or for the heroine and the hero.

Again, the attributes given above lean toward the development of a benign secondary character. The emotional makeup of a villain is developed by taking one or more attributes and grossly exaggerating them to the point of obsession.

For example, a gentleman who fears loss of face can be a fairly weak personality who is motivated by characters with stronger personalities than himself. He will be like a straw blown about by the wind, perhaps pressed into deep gaming by unsavory characters and thereafter resorts to silly machinations to put off the discovery of his embarrassing debts by his brother, the hero.

The fear of loss of face, grossly exaggerated and bestowed upon a gentleman of tarnished moral values, is a powerful motivator for villainous actions. This sort of gentleman will go to any lengths to preserve his public persona. He will lie, cheat, resort to physical violence; but never are these unpleasant techniques resorted to where there is the possibility of exposure. He works behind the scenes, manipulating others to his purposes, and when he does come out into the open it is always in circumstances that are advantageous to him. Whenever his mask is stripped aside, the resulting loss of face is unbearable.

In my book *The Righteous Rakehell*, the villain is a consummate gamester who unmercifully preys on others in order to strip them of their fortunes. His victims are left destitute and in despair. More than anything else, this gentleman fears the same fate he metes out to his "plucked pigeons". When he is at last bested at cards and loses everything, he is unable to bear the thought of life as a pauper. In the original manuscript, the villain shot himself, but my editor thought that too grisly an ending. Instead, the villain was allowed to flee to the Continent to live out the remainder of his life in miserable poverty. I still feel that the villain's original fate was more logical because his motivation was that strong. However, sometimes the writer must acquiesce graciously to the editor's taste and opinion and experience of the marketplace.

Character attributes, too, can be exaggerated in the same manner to provide villains with extreme motivation for their actions.

Character attributes:
1) kindliness or cruelty;
2) concern or indifference;

3) jealousy and envy;
4) obsession;
5) arrogance and hauteur;
6) pride or humility;
7) insecurities of one kind or another;
8) indecisive dithering, or decisive;
9) intelligent and cunning, or somewhat dense;
10) educated or uneducated;
11) tactful or tactless;
12) responsible or not (toward family, friends, reputation, honor);
13) honorable or dishonorable;
14) patient or impatient;
15) obstinate or malleable;
16) ruthless;
17) gaucherie or grace of manners;
18) aggressive, or shrinking, nature;
19) hasty, or even, temper
20) cheerful or gloomy;
21) good or evil.

Gross exaggerations of emotional and character attributes can work just as well in creating foolish, dependable, or humorous characters.

For example, a gentleman who is exceptionally tactless and not particularly intelligent is an admirable character to use in creating awkward and humorous circumstances for the heroine and the hero. He is a good sort and he wishes only the best for the heroine; but his attempts to help the heroine to snare the hero take the form of embarrassing confidences to the hero about the heroine and the orchestration of improper *tete-a-tetes*.

Since we have combined the character attributes for both female and male secondary characters, this list becomes very long. Attributes for both female and male secondary characters are also combined in the following.

Social attributes:
1) wealth or lack of;
2) good family or not (good family often determines
   whether this secondary character runs in the same
   social circles as the heroine and the hero);
3) graceful manners or a rude style;
4) ability to hold own in "manly" or "womanly" pursuits;
5) fashionable or unfashionable dress;

6) educated or uneducated tastes;
7) manner of speech - well-bred or vulgar;
8) commands liking and respect, or fear;
9) engenders contempt, ridicule or pity.

The social attributes chosen for the secondary characters should complement their emotional and character attributes. The secondary character's position in society, how he or she carries himself or herself, what their self-image is, and how they are perceived by the other characters is vital to the character's believability.

The primary attributes that provide motivation for the secondary characters or, indeed, any other, are emotional and character attributes. Social attributes are the underpinning and provide the frame that highlight the primary attributes. Physical attributes, such as beauty, or a handsome or fearsome appearance, should merely extend or emphasis the overall impression that is created by the primary attributes.

The writer is not to be limited by any list, but is free to build and mix and match for the combination that best describes the type of character that will aid the plot, or action, of the story. The point to keep in mind is that whatever attributes that the secondary characters are to be endowed with must somehow provide the tenor of the atmosphere whenever this character appears, and the motivations behind the character's actions and words.

For example, usher onto the stage a matron of common background who speaks her mind on however she perceives things to be, whose daughter is the object of a rakish gentleman's attentions and whom she is anxious to see off her hands so that she can wed again herself. She will be delighted that the rakish gentleman has presented himself and overly anxious that her daughter will make a lasting impression. Perhaps she does not particularly care whether her daughter is solicited as a wife or as a mistress. She fawns on the gentleman and practically pushes her daughter into his arms. Her appearance on the stage is likely to be on the humorous side, but at the same time her actions and her words have serious consequences for the heroine, who probably values her own virtue more highly than does her mother and who is humiliated by her mother's toadying overtures to the contemptuous gentleman.

Or, introduce a villain. He is bored beyond measure. He is wealthy and of impeccable lineage, but he is known to seduce young ladies. He takes notice of the heroine and his jaded interest is piqued. The heroine and her family alike spurn his advances. His ego is affronted, but it is no large matter, after all. Then it comes to his attention that the heroine is encouraging his arch-enemy, a gentleman much like him in social prominence but whose good character ensures him of welcome where the villain is given short shrift. Suddenly it becomes imperative that the villain have the heroine, willing or not. This gentleman's appearance onto the stage will always signal unease and apprehension, and even fear, on the heroine's part.

The secondary character can be friend or foe, a dispassionate player or an obsessed rogue, funny or sympathetic or fearsome. Whatever and whomever the secondary characters are, their job is to provide progression and growth to the story and to the evolving relationship between the heroine and the hero.

Secondary characters are not always human. Animals such as horses or dogs at times make excellent foils for the heroine and the hero. People have always held soft spots in their hearts for their favorite pets. It should not be any different between the pages of a book, especially one of romance which must as a matter of course explore the more tender emotions.

The secondary character may also be a natural phenomena, such as "old man winter", as long as the phenomena seems to provide uncannily human actions, or it can be brought to life and up to the human plain of experience through powerful description and the assignment of human characteristics. Examples of such characteristics might be malignant and evil weather, perverse tides, contrary and stubborn winds, etc., which would naturally have a bearing on the fortunes of a smuggler. Smuggling, by the way, was a major concern in Britain during the time that Napoleon Bonaparte banned all trade between France and England. It was not unheard of for noble families whose estates ran along the Dover coast to take part in such nefarious activity in order to enrich their coffers and their wine cellars.

The use of a natural phenomena as a secondary character is easier to do in a story about a less "sophisticated" society. For instance, in Hawaiian myth the goddess Pele was in actuality a rather active volcano. The volcano was personified and deified and therefore played a strong major roles in the lives of the people. When the natural phenomena is woven into the very fabric of the culture of the people, no one questions that the heroine and the hero can be highly motivated by this same phenomena.

The same effect is slightly more difficult to accomplish in the modern world. However, technology holds its own bugaboos. Many people are initially afraid of computers and what they think the machines can do. Computers are alien, smart, unrelated to human warmth or emotion. Until a person learns that a computer is a tool and only as efficient as its human programmers make it, the aura of the scary unknown remains.

The regency era saw a burgeoning of technological advances , some of which (like the spinning machine that mass-produced thread), created social disruptions in the form of destructive mobs. This in turn created a very real fear of revolution, revolution of the sort that had turned France into a bloodbath only twenty years before. Using such events as minor plot devices is entirely possible.

Another technological development dating from the period were the steam engines that ran on short spans of track. These monsters chuffed and puffed, frightening not only those who did not understand machines but the horses attached to their carriages as well. The technological bugaboo need not be central to the theme of the story, but may merely provide one sort of obstacle that must be overcome. Perhaps the heroine's horses bolt with her and she escapes serious injury only through the hero's quick intervention. When the heroine's father learns the name of his daughter's rescuer, he forbids her to have anything more to do with him because the gentleman is a financial backer of the steam engine, which the old man considers a "loathsome and hellish invention".

Anything that is bewildering, of the unknown, frightening, incomprehensible, impossible to explain - these things we human beings either find out the facts about or, if that isn't possible, we make up satisfying myths about them. It is part of our make-up that we cannot stand to have an unsolvable puzzle or mystery hanging about. Therefore, the viability of a natural phenomena as a secondary character should be kept in mind. It can and it has worked.

The secondary character may also be an historic event so central to the lives of the heroine and the hero, and to the direction of the story, that the story could not be told without it's inclusion. This might be a bloody battle and its outcome, an assassination attempt on a political figure, or the first staging of a particular and historically well-known stage performance.

Children are perhaps the most difficult secondary characters to employ. By their very nature, children require care and attention. That is as true in fiction as it is in life. A baby cannot simply be put in the nursery and forgotten until it is convenient for the heroine or the hero to remember it. Everyone knows that a baby needs feeding, changing, burping, cuddling, and bathing, and then it starts all over again. An older child is nearly as impossible as an infant to ignore during the unfolding of a story. A young boy cannot be ushered off-stage with the dash of a sentence explaining that he is taking a repairing lease from his creditors, as a more adult secondary character might be. Children just need attention, and if that logical and necessary requirement cannot be met without sacrificing the development of the relationship between the heroine and the hero, then these young and disruptive secondary characters must go.

On the flip side, a child can be a most compelling secondary character. A disruptive influence deluxe, a child instantly causes reactions among all of the cast and consequently to the movement of the plot. This secondary character must be utilized carefully with a deft hand, simply because a child is one of the most powerful characters available to the writer. The child secondary character will either strengthen the story wonderfully or weaken it disastrously.

Secondary male characters can be sexy, whether threateningly so or simply enough to confuse the heroine in her ultimate choice. However, remember that the hero is always *the* sexiest gentleman, bar none. The same goes for the heroine. She must be sexier and more appealing to the hero than any secondary female characters. If you have a secondary character that sizzles on the page and makes the heroine or the hero pale by comparison, either make that character one of the main players or get it matched up as quickly as possible with another character so as not to threaten the primary romance between the heroine and the hero.

Sometimes there develops a secondary character that is so wonderful, so sympathetic, so intriguing, that he or she overshadows not only the hero or the heroine, but even the romance. If a secondary character does this, extreme action must be taken: kill off the character, dilute it's impact by dividing it into two or more characters, lose it at sea or to the wiles of another secondary character.

If none of these methods work, then take a good hard look at the hero or the heroine - you may have mistaken who is supposed to star in the romantic roles. If this last is the case, ditch the original hero or heroine, (whichever is threatened by this wonderful secondary character), and replace him or her with the understudy who is so determined to steal the show. Go with your instincts and your gut feelings. The odds are that if you do, you will come out with a better book and at far less of a struggle.

Attempting to fight with a strong character is a futile exercise and can cost you time and even the willingness to stick to the writing of the book. It has been my experience that whenever the writing is most difficult, most tedious, and most awful, it is because I am attempting to coerce the characters into actions that run counter to the very attributes that I have given them.

Allow the characters to react as a result of their own unique attributes and you'll experience far less agony over the plot and how it is forming and flowing. Naturally, this means that whatever outline you began with will be altered in some degree or other as the book goes along. This is nothing to be upset about; rather, think of it as creativity in the making. There are few people who can think of every nuance of their story before they sit down to write it.

Chapter Seven

TITLES AND FORMS OF ADDRESS

In England, the nobility was known as the upper ten thousand, or, if a person wished to be even more selective, the Four Hundred.

There is a book called Burke's Peerage. Many city libraries have a copy of it. This tome is approximately six inches wide and is an exhaustive genealogical summation of British nobility. Burke's will state whether a British noble house was founded by a knight who came over with William the Conqueror in 1066 A.D., whether a particular duke also possesses other titles, what estates that duke possesses, whom married whom, etc. It is a mind-boggling collection of facts that serves to underscore the intermingling and intermarrying among the British nobility. It also points up the confusion that may arise if the writer is not familiar with titles and rules of descent in the nobility.

Titles and forms of address is a tricky topic and one loaded with unexpected traps. More than one writer has received letters from readers pointing up errors in title usage. Readers are very knowledgeable about such protocol and some are not shy in letting their favorite authors know it.

Titles and forms of address is such a prickly subject that Mary Jo Putney touched on it during a seminar at a romance writers' conference. Ms. Putney gave out handouts delineating the major pitfalls and I must acknowledge my debt to her for the bringing together of much of the following information.

Since the regency romance is centered upon English society, the emphasis here will be on the British nobility.

British titles are as follows in descending order of importance:

Duke	Duchess
Marquess	Marchioness
Earl	Countess *
Viscount	Viscountess
Baron	Baroness
Baronet	(none)
Knight	Dame

* The British earl is equivalent to the continental title of "count".

Dukes and duchesses are addressed differently than the others. The duke is formally addressed as "Your Grace" or "Sir"; informally, as "Duke". He is referred to as "the Duke of Wellington" or "His Grace of Wellington". Employees address him as "Your Grace" and refer to him as "His Grace". The duchess is formally addressed as "Your Grace" or "Madam", and informally as "Duchess". She is referred to as "the Duchess of Wellington" or "Her Grace of Wellington". Her maid addresses her as "Your Grace" and refers to her as "Her Grace".

The marquess, the earl, the viscount and the baron are referred to in conversation as "Lord Hazard". The use of their exact rank is incorrect in a social setting, unless for some reason it must be specifically mentioned. At a formal function, the exact title may be given at first mention of the peer, such as when the gentleman is announced to the gathered company upon his arrival. After that initial introduction, he again becomes "Lord Hazard". These peers are addressed as "my lord".

The marchioness, the countess, and the viscountess are referred to as "Lady Hazard". Again, use of the exact rank is incorrect unless the lady is being introduced into formal company upon her arrival. These ladies are addressed as "my lady". Employees address these peers and their ladies as "my lord" and "my lady", but refer to them as "his lordship" and "her ladyship".

Dowgers are widows whose sons have attained to the title. They are referred to as "Dowger Duchess of Avon", "Dowger Marchioness of..", "Dowger Countess of..", and are addressed the same way they were before their widowhood. In other words, they are still addressed as "Lady Hazard".

The son who has inherited his father's title need not be married before his mother is referred to as "Dowger".

A baron is never referred to as "Baron Rathbone" or "the baron". The title of baron is only used on legal documents or in formal correspondence. This peer is always addressed as "Lord Rathbone". He is called "my lord" by acquaintances. His servants address him as "my lord" and refer to him as "his lordship".

The baronet is formally addressed as "Sir Charles Rathbone". In an informal gathering, he is addressed as "Sir Charles".

The baroness, the wife of a baronet, or the wife of a knight are all addressed as "Lady Rathbone" or as "my lady". Servants address these ladies as "my lady" and refer to them as "her ladyship".

An individual would not address another of equal standing as "His lordship" or "Her ladyship", unless in the presence of a servant. A lord might say to a footman, "His lordship has finished his wine-bring more." However, if two nobles are discussing another noble, they can refer to the absent party as "his lordship" or as "Lord Kenelm".

In narration and indirect address, the title appears in lower case, (i.e., "The duke came to the party.") However, the title appears in upper case when the peer is specifically named, (i.e., "She knew it was the Duke of Dalby.") This form holds true for all titles except for the Prince Regent or the Prince Consort, which, even without proper name, is always in upper case.

Dukes, marquesses, earls, viscounts, and barons are peers. Their titles are hereditary and they sit in the House of Lords. The title baron is the lowest order of the nobility; in the absence of sons, a few baronies can pass to daughters.

Baronets are not peers, but yet their titles are hereditary. Baronets are commoners and they may sit in the House of Commons, if elected. Baronet is the lowest rank of inherited title; if there is no son, some baronetcies can pass to a daughter.

Knights and dames are also commoners and their titles of honor are not hereditary. These titles are bestowed upon the recipients by the king or the queen in recognition of meritorious service or accomplishment. Many British performers in the arts have been so honored. Examples: Dame Margot Fontaigne, Dame Agatha Christie, Dame Barbara Cartland, Sir Lawrence Olivier, and Sir Rex Harrison.

Squires are rich country gentlemen without titles.

Courtesy titles are carried by the children of the upper nobility. The holders of these courtesy titles are considered commoners, even though their parents are noble. Even the heir to the peerage is a commoner; but he has a courtesy title, which is usually his father's second highest title.

The most common error committed by the unwary writer is to use "Lord" or "Lady" with a first name, such as "Lord John" or "Lady Mary". "Lord John" would be the courtesy title used *only* by the younger son of a duke or a marquess. The daughter of a duke, of a marquess or of an earl *only* would be addressed as "Lady Mary".

Peers often possess more than one title and the higher in the hierarchy the peer is placed, the more junior titles he is likely to have. For instance, our character is the Marquess of Devon, the Earl of Kenelm, Viscount Allyn. The eldest son of the marquess takes his father's junior title, usually that of earl. He is known as "the Earl of Kenelm", or "Lord Kenelm". The marquess's second-born son, who is not the heir, is known by the family surname and is addressed as "Lord Alexander" or "Lord Alexander Carstairs".

In the upper levels of the aristocracy, the grandson and eventual heir to the peerage may also carry a courtesy title, usually the peer's third highest title. For example, the Marquess of Devon's grandson, who is also the Earl of Kenelm's oldest son, would be "Viscount Allyn" and would be addressed as "Lord Allyn". When the Marquess of Devon dies, everyone moves up a notch. The earl becomes the new marquess and a noble. The grandson becomes the new Earl of Kenelm, but since the title is one of courtesy the new earl is still a commoner.

The first-born son, (or the son of a deceased oldest son), who is heir to the title is called the "heir apparent" because, unless he dies before his father, he will inherit. If he is the heir of a duke, a marquess, or an earl, he will carry a courtesy title until such time as he actually inherits the peerage.

If the heir to a title is a nephew, or other male relative who is not a son, he is the "heir presumptive". This means that his claim to the title can be superseded by the birth of a direct male heir, a son. For instance, the Marquess of Devon has no sons and his heir is his younger brother's son, his nephew. If the widowed Marquess of Devon suddenly remarries and his young wife produces a son, the nephew is no longer the marquess's heir. The "heir presumptive" does not carry a courtesy title as does the heir to a title. Instead, how he is known is determined by his own father's lesser rank, in this case, "Lord Carstairs".

The eldest son of an earl takes his father's junior title, usually viscount. He is "Viscount Allyn" and is addressed as "Lord Allyn". The younger son of an earl is known by the family name, as in "the Honorable Edward Carstairs" and is addressed as "Mister Edward Carstairs".

All male peers except dukes are addressed by their last name preceded by "Lord". A peer is properly referred to as "Richard, Lord Carruthers" or "Lord Carruthers". He is a noble in his own right. A peer is never called "Lord Richard Carruthers" or "Lord Richard", which would mean that he was the younger son of a duke or marquess and therefore a commoner.

In the upper ranks of the British nobility, sisters outrank their brothers by one degree. All daughters of an earl are addressed as "Lady Mary", "Lady Agatha", and so on, while those of their brothers who are not the heir are "the Honorable". In most Continental countries, the children of nobles are nobles themselves and often carry their father's rank. For instance, the children of a prince are all addressed as "prince" or"princess".

The children of viscounts and barons, like the younger sons of earls, are known as "the Honorable Charles Ledbetter" or "the Honorable Eudora Ledbetter". However, they are never introduced as "honorables"; rather, they are addressed as "Mister Charles Ledbetter" and "Miss Eudora Ledbetter", the latter of which is the eldest daughter of the family. Younger daughters are addressed by their first names, such as "Miss Flora" and "Miss Mary". The heirs of viscounts and barons are referred to as "the Honorable", like their younger brothers and sisters.

The children of baronets or knights do not have a courtesy title, not even "Honorable". They are addressed as "Mister" and "Miss".

Within the British nobility, the children of peers and peeresses are not considered noble unless they inherit, or marry, a title. With the exception of daughters of the nobility, (such as the daughter of royalty, or of a duke, a marquess, or an earl), women receive titles only through marriage.

Women whose husbands are marquesses, earls, viscounts, barons or baronets are addressed by their surnames preceded by "Lady", or as "my lady".

Lady Mary Kenelm is a commoner, though she is the daughter of an earl. If she marries a commoner, such as Sir Thomas Beckenham, she combines her husband's family name with her courtesy title and becomes "Lady Mary Beckenham".

If Lady Mary marries a man with a title, she will assume her husband's title if it is higher than hers. For instance, if her husband is the Marquess of Monty, she becomes the Marchioness of Monty and is addressed as "Lady Monty".

If Lady Mary marries Lord Alistar Randolph, the younger son of the Marquess of Monty, she takes her husband's name and she is addressed as "Lady Alistar Randolph" or "Lady Alistar". In this instance, she would never be called "Lady Randolph", which would imply that her husband was a peer; nor would she be addressed as "Lady Mary", which was her given name.

A woman who has no connections to the peerage is addressed as "Miss Elizabeth Addams". If she marries Lord Petersall, she becomes "Lady Petersall". She is not ever addressed as "Lady Elizabeth" because that would imply that she was the daughter of a duke, a marquess, or an earl.

Another example of marrying up would be that of the real-life Lady Diana Spencer, who is the daughter of the Earl of Spencer. Before she married, she was addressed as "Lady Diana"; she was never referred to as "Lady Spencer" because that would be her mother or her sister-in-law. When Lady Diana married Charles, the Prince of Wales, she did not become "Princess Di", as she is popularly called in the media. This is incorrect and implies that she was born to the rank of princess. Queen Elizabeth's sister, Princess Anne, is called by her first name because she was born to the rank. Instead, she became Diana, Princess of Wales.

When a woman remarries, she adopts the rank of her husband, even if it is lower than her own. For example, Mary, Duchess of Avon, marries Mr. John Matthews and becomes Mrs. John Matthews.

However, if the woman has a courtesy title from her father, she will revert to this on remarriage. Perhaps this woman was the daughter of an earl and was known as Lady Mary Hope, becoming upon her marriage to the Duke of Avon, the Duchess of Avon. Later, when she married Mr. John Matthews, she became Lady Mary Matthews. Or, if she was the daughter of a viscount and was known as the "Honorable Mary Hope" before her first marriage to the duke, upon her remarriage to Mr. John Matthews she would become the Honorable Mrs. Matthews.

Proper protocol also exists in written forms of address. This naturally does not appear often in a book, but occasionally the heroine receives a missive from the hero, and though the entire message is not given the reader, the hero's signature is always remarked upon.

When a peer sets down his signature, he does not write "The Marquess of Devon"; "The Earl of Kenelm'"; "Viscount Allyn"; or even "Lord Carstairs". He writes "Devon"; "Kenelm"; "Allyn"; or "Carstairs".

If the heroine wishes to invite the hero to her soiree, her note is addressed to him making full use of his title, as in "The Marquess of Devon", et. al.

A formal letter to the hero would begin, "My lord", and end, "Yours faithfully". If the hero is a close acquaintance, the letter would begin on a more social note, as in "Dear Lord Carstairs", and would end, "Yours sincerely".

When creating identities for the characters, it is probably best not to use an actual and existent title. I remember reading in a biography of Georgette Heyer that she once landed in some difficulty for borrowing an actual peerage name for one of her characters. The peer whose name she had used was not amused that his illustrious title had appeared in a work of fiction. Thereafter Ms. Heyer used geographical place names and the names of towns for inspiration in creating titles for her characters. Title names can of course be created whole out of the writer's imagination or created by taking parts of existent titles to mix and match.

Protocol and hierarchy are also quite rigid among the ranks of those employed by the aristocracy, as well. The never-never land that exists between the family and the servants is inhabited by the personal secretary, the personal companion, and the governess.

The personal secretary is generally a gentleman. He is the confidante of the master of the house and sometimes even trods the fine line of friendship. His employer refers to him by his surname, as "Thorne". Servants address the secretary as "Mr. Thorne".

The personal companion, or hired companion, is generally a middle-aged female of gentle birth who had to support herself. Her job is to act not only as companion to the mistress of the house, but also as her ladyship's personal secretary and general gopher. She is also occasionally called upon to absorb whatever ill-temper or abuse that her mistress feels inclined to dispense. The personal companion is often in her ladyship's confidence and, at best, is treated as an uncritical friend. The personal companion might be a poor relation that her ladyship has befriended by giving her such a position, in which case her salary may very well consist of bed-and-board and cast-off clothing. She is addressed by either her given name or her surname, depending upon the degree of friendliness that her ladyship allows in their relationship. The personal companion might eat at table with the family or she might take her meals in her room.

The governess is of equal rank with the personal companion, in that she often serves in that capacity as well as in her own. She teaches the children of the house and may also serve as her ladyship's personal secretary, companion, and gopher. She is usually addressed as "Miss Appleby", but sometimes the mistress of the house may establish a warmer relationship with her and address her by her given name. The governess does not join the family at dinner, but takes her meals in the nursery.

The butler and the housekeeper are the highest-ranking servants. The butler is referred to by his surname, as in "Smythe". The housekeeper is referred to as "Mrs. Hodges". Sometimes the butler and housekeeper are husband-and-wife, which in this case makes them "Smythe" and "Mrs. Smythe".

His lordship's valet and her ladyship's dresser are of superior rank to the butler and housekeeper. The valet is usually referred to by his surname and so is the dresser, as in "Waters" and "Greene". Sometimes her ladyship, addresses her dresser by the woman's given name, if mistress and servant have a long and affectionate history.

The cook is addressed as "Mrs. Peabody" or "Cook" or , if the tyrant of the kitchen is an expensive Gallic chef, as "Monsieur Bonault".

Footmen, parlor maids, upstairs maids, and scullery maids are all addressed by their given names. If a footman is fortunate enough to eventually rise to the position of butler, he is thereafter referred to by his surname. Similarly, if an ordinary maid is one day given her chance to become a lady's maid, she is also addressed thereafter by her surname.

Outside the house, the servants also have their own protocol and hierarchy. The groundskeeper is addressed by his surname, while the gardeners under him are addressed by their given names. The gameskeeper is addressed by his surname. The master of the stable is addressed as "Tibbs"; the stablehands under his supervision are addressed by their given names.

For greater detail regarding servants and their protocol, etc., please refer to reference books on housekeeping of the period.

This short dissertation should provide enough of a guideline that the most blatant errors in providing blue-blood characters with pedigrees and servants with proper monikers can be sidestepped. As you become more experienced and familiar with the use of titles and forms of address, it will become second nature to you. But do not let a lack in this area of knowledge discourage you. For now, just keep the story rolling. This is a technical area that can be modified or corrected later.

Chapter Eight

RESEARCH

Every endeavor demands preparation, whether it is training for a 10K race or whipping up a special dinner or writing a book. Preparation equals research, if you will.

According to the dictionary, research is "scholarly or scientific investigation or inquiry". This is a very limited definition for our purposes, because I believe that personal observation is as much a part of research as is digging through musty-smelling historical documents.

In order to write about believable characters, you must have an idea of how people react to certain things. Quietly watch people at the park or in the car next to yours while at the traffic light. Really look at your family and friends when they are talking or playing. Observe their expressions and their body language, their actions and their reactions. Catch a sentence or two as you walk past some strangers loitering at the store counter or at the bus stop. Indulge yourself and listen, really listen, to the stories that old people tell and to the funny questions that kids ask. Look at what people are wearing, what they own, and what they don't.

All of these things tell you something about those people and their lives, what they might think about themselves and others, what they believe in and what they think is a crock. You often learn what is important to them and what isn't simply by an off-hand comment or a shrug of the shoulders or an emphatic shake of the head.

People-watching is very informative. It is this basic research that will enable the writer to capture mannerisms, speech patterns, character attributes, social attributes and emotional attributes. You begin to learn what motivates people to act as they do, and this is basic to true character development and conflict. Anyone who is successful in the acting profession will have immersed themselves into this kind of research many times over to be able to convincingly depict whatever roles they have taken on.

Hands-on personal experience of a trade or a profession, of handling life's crisis' and joys - this, too, is a form of research. We are all constantly learning and constantly changing, or having change forced upon us. We adapt or cave in; surpass, excel, or fail. Through it all, we experience every possible emotion under the sun. How we act or react personally to changing circumstances, or even to a stagnating situation, puts us through life's gauntlet time and again. This boiling pot is an incredible source of information for developing character motivation. This is research you've already done. It's there in your head, ready to be tapped.

Though people-watching is observation of contemporary people in contemporary times, it is still relevant even to the writing of a book set in the Ice Ages, as we've seen in Jean Auel's *Clan of the Cave Bears*. Human emotions, hopes and fears have remained constant and universal throughout the ages. Emotions, hopes and fears are tempered by the structure and the culture and the age that the people's lives are bounded by, but basics remain the same:

> Love, hope, loneliness, caring;
> fear of vulnerability, risk, loss;
> sense of belonging, comfort, alienation;
> survival, conquest, freedom, flight, struggle, etc.

It has been said over and over, write what you know. Get to know people and you can virtually write about anything else you want to, whether fiction or non-fiction, because scholarly or scientific research provide merely the dry bones of what makes up human concerns. It is what goes on in people's minds and hearts that clothe those bones and give them animation.

Scholarly research for the regency period is exceptionally easy. The Regency was a specific period of English history, beginning in 1811 and ending in 1820. These years serve as the boundaries to the research required for a regency romance. Any historical detail that falls outside these boundaries cannot be used; In other words, the writer has automatically built in a brake by choosing the Regency era for the story's setting. The sometimes devastatingly difficult decision about whether to use a particular historical fact or to discard it is already made in some instances and this saves the writer time.

The Regency period came about when King George III went insane in 1810 and was no longer capable of his monarchial functions. His son, the Prince of Wales, was named the Prince Regent in 1811 and took over governing the kingdom. George III did not die until 1820; at his death, the Prince Regent was crowned King George IV, ending the regency.

The Regency period lasted nine years. That is only nine years that a writer must look at to gather details for the background of a regency romance. The writer, especially the beginner who has not yet trained herself to know when to stop researching and begin writing, is less likely to become bogged down by the sheer mass of historical material available when the historical period is this narrow.

Points to consider and include in the process of researching for a regency romance include:

1) fashion - clothes, hairstyles, headgear, trimmings, undergarments;
2) language - speech patterns, including popular and vulgar slang;
3) setting - London townhouse, country estate, foreign shores; shops, men's clubs, coffee houses, lending library, theaters, etc.;
4) furniture and furnishings; wood types, upholstery, fabrics, design; bric-a-brac, paintings, carpets, clocks, mirrors;
5) architecture - inside and outside of a typical townhouse or of a country manor house, Carlton House or other well-known historical place, bridges, gas lighting in the streets, etc.;
6) food and drink - what could be expected at any particular meal, including holidays; documented idiosyncrasies of actual historical figures; types of wine preferred at different times of day by different social groups; popularity of French *haut cuisine*;
7) carriages - style of, speed of , color of; number of horses required; number of passengers possible;
8) social mores - hand-kissing, bows, curtsies; ladies leaving the gentlemen alone to enjoy their after dinner wine; cigar-smoking, snuff-taking;
9) medicine, toiletries, and cosmetics;
10) favored reading, scandalous reading (Byron, Keats, Wordsworth, Austen);
11) favored theater productions (opera, Shakespeare, ballet);

    favored performers (Siddons, Kean, Vestris, Cataloni, Kemble, Grimaldi);

12) what was proper behavior, what was not; chaperones, intimacies, gifts; social restrictions (for women, in particular);

13) entertainments - hot-air balloon ascensions, Astley's Circus, Almacks', sporting events;

14) politics - the Peninsular War, naval battles, the Battle of Waterloo, the Congress of Vienna, war with the American colonies; trade questions (i.e., smuggling and Napoleon's embargo against England); social unrest and the fear of revolution.

Naturally, all of this information cannot possibly be fitted into any single regency romance. However, by becoming familiar with the period and what was going on internationally as well as on the home front, the writer will be able to include the touches of authenticity that are as much a part of the regency romance as the love story. It is very important to be able to command some knowledge of the above areas, or at least to know where to find some particular tidbit, because the setting and the tone of the story is essential to its success as a regency. In addition, this pool of research will often suggest new story lines to pursue.

For instance, you have decided to give the hero an interesting scar from a wound that he received during the Battle of Waterloo. That battle was fought in June, 1815; therefore, the story takes place sometime between 1816 and 1820. These are then the years that you look at for fashions in clothing, the hottest trends in furniture and furnishings, etc. The writer can literally pinpoint the year, the season, the month, sometimes even the day of the week, (for example, Almacks' subscription balls were held on Wednesday evenings), that the story takes place.

And so can your readers.

Readers read regencies because they very much enjoy that particular historical period. They are familiar with the background and the social graces and the young lady's hopes of making an eligible marriage. They know about the Peninsular War and the Battle of Waterloo. They know about poke bonnets and high-waisted gowns. They know about the prestige of receiving the coveted vouchers to Almacks'. They are comfortable with the forms of address and the social protocol used then.

Regency romance readers do catch the results of negligent research that even the author or the publishing house might let slip past. These readers will write the author and the publishing house about the mistakes, too. They dash off letters expressing dismay that a perfectly good story fell disappointingly flat for them because they discovered that they knew more than the author about the regency period.

This sort of feedback can be viewed as intimidating. However, keep in mind that the readers of regency romances are loyal and appreciative. They positively love regency romances. Some of them won't read anything else. Whatever else happens in the up-and-down publishing business, there is always a steady core audience devoted to regency romances.

Sources to mine for good regency material abound. It was a prolific period in more than one sense. There was a flowering of the arts and architecture, in cabinet-making, and in industrial advances. Social restlessness caused by the industrial revolution was contributed to by the uncertainty created by the waging of war on two fronts.

This turbulence was reflected in the volume of available sources. Memoirs, the Duke of Wellington's Military Dispatches, Jane Austen's novels, newspapers and magazines dating from the period, etc., will give the writer an immediate sense of place, an idea of what was happening, and a feel for the language. Other good sources are biographies of individuals whose lives included the regency period. Reference books on nearly every topic that you could possibly wish are available at the public libraries.

By the way, books that include reproductions of fine prints or paintings done during the regency period are invaluable because the writer can actually see what the people wore; see what the buildings and streets looked like; and examine details of some of the entertainments that they enjoyed, such as horse races or pugilistic spectacles. A description of the inside of a haberdashers shop or the lending library is helpful; but to see reproductions of prints of these places allows the writer to observe fine details that another's description might fail to include. These minute details scattered into the prose of the story will convey the essential touch of authenticity that is so vital to the regency romance, or, for that matter, to any other historical novel.

These reference sources can be gotten from the public library or the bookstore. If there is a specific book that the writer simply must consult but can't readily find, it can often be obtained through inter-library loan. This service allows books to be pulled from libraries across the country and back, and most librarians are more than willing to aid you in your research in this fashion.

An all-inclusive "must" list of reference books is impossible to compile. The vast amount of material available is simply too overwhelming. However, below is a listing of subject headings that at any library will open up specific titles and other topic headings for the Regency period. In addition, the appendix lists some specific titles relating to some of these various topics.

Peninsular War
Waterloo, Battle of
Brussels (Belgium capitol where all of European high society
        awaited the outcome of the Battle of Waterloo)
British history, 1800-1820
Wellington, Duke of
George III
George IV
Congress of Vienna (Peace negotiations after Napoleon's
        abdication; again all of European high society gathered in
        this capitol to await outcome.)
George Nash, architect
Jane Austen, novelist
Costume, 19th century
Herbs, Formal Gardens
Architecture - British, French, European, Russian
Furniture
Religion - Anglican, Catholic; marriage customs
Industrial Revolution
Carriages, Coaches, Vehicles
Cosmetics
Customs - British; holidays
Cooking - British and French
Memoirs - by military gentlemen; by visitors to London, to Russia,
        to Brussels, to Vienna, and the rest of Europe. Look under
        the specific country's historical headings.
Dictionaries - slang usage (believe it or not, there are
        dictionaries devoted strictly to slang)
Housekeeping - reference books dating from or around
        the regency period that go into what tasks the servants
        are required to do, what their wages were, table settings,
        menus, home remedies, etc.

I have at one time or another consulted books from each of these categories. Often, I have used several references for a single story. For instance, for *Lord John's Lady*, I read memoirs written by English travelers to Russia and the memoirs of English compatriots who lived and worked in Russia. I consulted studio books that pictured architectural forms of great Russian palaces and stately French chateaus. I also read books about London entertainments of the period. All of these were in addition to the usual peeks at costume books and references to carriages.

I have attempted to find out about anything that the heroine or the hero needed to know to make the story develop properly, or that they would have taken for granted within the fabric of their lives.

This list is not inclusive, of course, of what is available. It is merely a starting point. Your particular story may hinge upon some little-known fact that has captured your imagination, but which might have been passed over before by dozens of regency writers before you. That is the beauty of imagination. The same body of research can be presented to ten different writers and at least ten different stories will arise out of it.

As you peruse reference material about the regency period, do not be surprised if your next story leaps out of the pages at you.

Chapter Nine

DESCRIPTION IN THE STORY

Description is imperative in any good story, but perhaps in none so much as an historical. Writing about any time different from our own automatically demands the inclusion of all sorts of information that we would not think of including in a contemporary story. In a historical, fascinating material might include a description of bathing in a hip-bath that is filled from copper pots or how a corset is laced up. In a contemporary, the modern bathtub or the lacy demi-bra do not need much space on the page.

The regency romance, by its very nature, must include sufficient description to enable the reader to feel at home in the Regency era. Description is what gets a reader truly involved in the story. Historical detail to illustrate every possible facet of a character's life may not actually be used in the final story, but the writer needs to know as much as possible to give the reader the flavor of that character's surroundings. Style of dress, furniture and furnishings, architecture, type of carriages, food and drink, et. al., are all important props in placing the character, and the reader, firmly into an historical background.

However, proper historical research is but one ingredient of good description. Really good description puts all five senses to work in the story. Often, description is limited to how things *appear* to the characters. But the characters should also have an awareness of their surroundings through *taste*, *touch*, *scent*, and *hearing*.

An ordinary ballroom scene might be described through the heroine's eyes as a crowd of smartly dressed gentlemen and lovely-gowned ladies, the latter aglitter with jewels. Some of the guests move leisurely about greeting one another. Some are dancing, while others take their ease in clusters of well-grouped chairs or play cards in the anterooms. The reader can see the scene.

Now, focus a little harder. The orchestra music is nearly drowned by frequent laughter and the loud din of conversation. As the heroine weaves her way through the crowd, she is jostled by a gentleman who instantly apologizes upon realizing his inadvertent transgression. Moving on again, snatches of conversation come to her ears. Beneath the blazing candelabras the heat of the room is unbearable and the scent of the overabundant flowers is nauseatingly strong. The heroine makes her way to the refreshment table for a lemon ice and gratefully slakes her parched throat.

The heroine has seen the ballroom, she has heard the noise, she has felt the jostling and the heat, she has smelled the overpowering scent of the flowers, and she has tasted the lemon ice. The heroine has experienced the ballroom scene in depth, and so has the reader.

Also notice that there are two ways to add description to a scene: using a wide angle lens or zeroing in on something small. The initial or opening description of the ballroom is a general impression of the whole. As the heroine moves through the crowd, the description narrows in on the gentleman who jostles her and his subsequent apology. The description widens its focus again to touch on unrelated pieces of conversation, the heat and the scent of the flowers, then is followed by a narrower focus on the heroine's reaction to a cool drink.

Description, then, is not simply relating a chain of dry observations. Decide what the scene is supposed to convey - the tone or mood of the setting and the action that is to take place. In the above description, the heroine is hot, thirsty, and unattached to any party or individual. She is certainly not enjoying herself. This has set the tone of the scene. Next would come the action, which would naturally begin with bringing another character to the heroine's notice. How the heroine reacts to that character, and that character to her, will become the action, and the point, of the scene.

An important tool to master in putting together an entertaining story is transition. Transition is an abridged form of description. It is the technique of gracefully telling the reader that a new act is about to begin, and generally in a new location.

Often the problem of getting a character from one scene to another seems insurmountable because of all the intervening detail that must be gotten through. For example, the hero has been enjoying a bout of fisticuffs at Jackson's Saloon. He is sweaty, his hair is tousled, his chin has been grazed by a well-placed fist. How is the hero conveyed from the boxing ring to the ballroom without going into exhaustive detail of his ambling home, taking a bath, dressing, eating dinner and whatever else seems required?

This sort of long involved description serves no good purpose. Instead, it slows down the story to an excruciating crawl. This in turn threatens the level of interest that the reader has developed in the story. A simple transition spans the distance: After leaving the saloon, the hero made his way home to ready himself for the ball that evening. Three hours later, immaculately turned out in evening coat and pantaloons, the hero entered the ballroom

Through the transition, the reader can easily infer that the hero bathed and changed his clothing and generally transformed himself into the sort of well-groomed gentleman that any heroine would be happy to dance with. The transition took up the space of two sentences in all to convey a change of activity, appearance, and location. The story is able to go on without a pause.

Notice that the transition also informed the reader of the passage of time. Marking the passage of time in this painless manner is easily the most important use of the transition. In order to maximize this particular usage of the transition, focus on physical action, (in this case, the hero's exit from the boxing saloon and his walk home), make note of any changes in the character's environment, (which might be the hero's awareness of the setting sun and the subsequent cooling of the air that heralds evening), and description of changes in the character's appearance and mannerisms, (for instance, the hero's impeccable manners upon greeting his hostess might serve in direct contrast to a previous description of his fierce joy as he landed a facer to his sparring partner.)

One of the simplest ways to show a lapse in time is to make note of the arrival of food and drink and its subsequent consumption by the characters. You must be careful how this is used, though, because the prose very readily becomes stilted if every snatch of dialogue is emphasized by the observation that the heroine had now finished one course and had begun on the next. Instead, slide in unobtrusive references to the food and drink that actually work to enhance the overall atmosphere of the scene.

For example, the heroine stared at her soup, unable to finish it. The footman removed the soup bowl and served the fowl onto her plate, but she did not think that she would be able to choke down even a mouthful after what she had just heard from the gentleman seated opposite. "You do not eat, my lady," he observed, as he poured another glass of wine for himself.

It is obvious that time has elapsed since this couple first sat down to dinner. The soup is generally served as a first course. The heroine was unable to finish it. The second course, the fowl, has begun. The gentleman poured himself another glass of wine. The reader infers the passing of time when words connoting past action are used, like "unable to finish" and "another".

The description of emotions is necessary to get the reader truly involved in the character's story. The rule of thumb is to show, not tell. If the writer shows how a character feels by what is going on, (much like a play might), then the reader feels like a participant in the story. Once the reader accepts this illusion, the book becomes impossible to put down. There are three ways of describing the characters' emotions. First, the writer may simply state it: She was so angry. Secondly, the character could show it through action: She snatched up the vase and threw it against the wall, shattering it. Lastly, the character could announce it: "I am so angry that I could scream!"

The best way to describe emotions is to illustrate them. When the writer does not illustrate the emotions of the characters, she becomes the narrator and intrudes herself between the reader and the characters. This intrusion forces the reader to draw back from full involvement with the characters.

However, this is not to say that by simply stating what a character is feeling cannot be used successfully. It can, especially when used in conjunction with an illustrative form. For example: She was so angry. She snatched up the vase and threw it against the wall, shattering it. "I am so angry I could scream!"

For the sake of bald clarity, the same exact sentences are used to illustrate the point. This scene actually has the potential for greater description, perhaps as follows: She was so angry. She fairly shook with fury. Her breast heaving, she stood with her hands clenched at her sides. Suddenly she darted to the mantle, snatched up the vase and threw it against the wall, shattering it. Enunciating each word quite deliberately, she said, "I am so angry I could scream!"

The description of an emotion should have a ripple effect. Toss the character's feelings into the pond, or scene, and envision what form the ripples take. What does the character say and how does he or she say it? What body language best illustrates the feelings? What physical action is set into motion? What are the reactions of any other characters involved?

These are the ripples. Anchor the emotions with this kind of description and the character's feelings come across with vivid impact.

Making use of the five senses is paramount to getting the reader involved in the story, but there are other techniques just as important. Dialogue and action often show the character to better advantage than will an otherwise passive description.

The hero sprawled in his chair, half-turned from the green baize game table, his cards held carelessly in one hand. The sudden droop of his heavy lids hid the expression in his eyes from his companions. His voice was dangerously soft. "Am I to understand that you suspect me of cheating, my lord?"

This description reads better than the following. The hero sat in his chair with his legs outthrust. He was half-turned from the green baize game table and he held his cards in one hand. None of his companions could read the expression in his eyes because his lids had drooped over them. He was angered by his lordship's insinuation that he had cheated.

This scene does not contain a great deal of inherent action, nor dialogue. However, the first description uses words like "sprawled" and "carelessly" to *show* how the hero is sitting. The action in the scene consists of a mere droop of the eyelids, but in the first example it is shown as it is happening (present tense) and in the second, it has already happened (past tense). In the first example, the hero's anger is illustrated, or shown, by how he speaks - "dangerously soft" - and the reason for his anger is conveyed through his own words. In the second example the writer *tells* the reader that the hero is angry and also why he feels that way.

The viewpoint from which the story is told impacts on how character emotions are described. Unlike the heroine and the hero, non-viewpoint characters rarely think about how they feel. Instead, they show it by what they say or do. The character's words convey emotion, opinion, and observation, all of which show something about the character. The character's movements enhance whatever the reader learned about him through his words, or even show that his actual feelings are contrary to what he has just said.

As an example of the latter, the secondary character may say to the hero, "The play was deep last night, but my losses were of little consequence." He moved restlessly in his chair, his eyes sliding away from the hero's thoughtful gaze.

Another use of description is that, through it, the writer is able to control the pace of the story. Long descriptive passages tend to slow the story. Short, brief descriptive snatches make the story pick up speed. Both techniques are fundamental in establishing the attributes of a character, the mood of a particular scene, and the tension of the book.

Slowing down the pace enables the reader to absorb minutia that otherwise might never be included in the fabric of the story. Small details convey parts and pieces that enhance the kind of atmosphere that the writer is trying to establish. For example, a description of the heroine's dress might be quite simple: She wore a modest round gown.

However, a lengthier description might convey a good deal more: There was nothing remarkable about her appearance. She wore a modest round gown made of gray merino that, with its high-cut bodice and long narrow sleeves, effectively disguised whatever figure she possessed. The description does not detail every article of the heroine's clothing, (which *is* sometimes done to show just how gorgeous she is on the eve of a special party, for instance), yet it conveys enough that the reader knows exactly what this heroine looks like to the hero at this particular moment. The lengthier description also gives notice that the interaction that will follow will do so at a rather sedate pace.

Short, swift snatches of description trumpet that the story is going to charge ahead, as in the following example: He whipped up the horses. The old carriage bowled faster over the road. The wind snatched at his hat, tearing it from his head. "Stop, stop!" she screamed. He laughed maniacally. (Notice, too, that the actual word count of the sentences also contributes to pace. Long sentences slow down the story; short sentences speed it up.) Here there is no mention of the gentleman's showy waistcoat or the hard glitter in his eyes or that he is unusually tall. These details are not needed. The description of the action is the important point, and it is swift and succinct. Yet here, too, the reader gets a very definite picture of this gentleman. He is obviously not a prudent nor a particularly nice man. The reader naturally wants to find out what happens next and why the heroine is in the company of such a disturbing gentleman. The pace of the story will slow in order to answer these questions and to further the tension that is being built through the interaction between these characters.

It is important to realize the power of description when used in this way. Controlling the pace of the story through description even establishes the difference between genres, such as differentiating a regency romance from a western. Both the regency and the western are set in historical contexts. Both use long and short descriptive passages. However, the tension level of a western is much higher than what one expects to find in a regency romance.

The difference, besides the obvious one of content (romance versus action), lays heavily on the way description is used. In a regency romance, there is a greater proportion of long descriptive passages because such things as romance and fashion lend themselves better to that form of description. A romantic interlude builds tension by dwelling on a languorous kiss and the characters' emotions. In a western, short descriptions abound, providing jolts of tension: The hero slapped leather. His gun came up blazing. The villain teetered on his toes, his gun hanging from his fingers. An astonished expression entered his hard eyes. Then he sprawled on his face.

Whatever the genre, the point of the book must be kept in mind. This determines the proportion of long to short descriptive passages that are used to move the story from beginning to end. Regency romances move steadily forward. The stories are full of detail, true; but the short descriptive passage is absolutely necessary if the reader is not to be deadened.

The heroine slapped the hero's face. His eyes blazing, he caught her wrist. "You will regret that, my lady!" This is short and descriptive. It has tension. It moves the story by providing conflict between the characters, much like what might be found in a western.

A western uses long descriptive passages to give the reader a breather from the tension produced by confrontation after confrontation. The regency romance uses short descriptive passages as heighteners of a slower-built tension formed through the longer passages.

The regency romance by definition is virtually guaranteed to contain several long descriptive passages. The wealth of historical detail, which is a staple of the genre, could not otherwise be showcased. The romantic interludes, also, would tend to shrink in importance if some attention was not spared to detail. However, do remember that a story captures reader interest because it goes someplace. Move the story by chopping up the descriptive passages with others that are oriented to dialogue and action.

Pages and pages of description guarantees the loss of reader interest. Today, we are conditioned to short TV news stories and to brief magazine articles that can be read in less than five minutes. A book naturally takes longer to absorb, but nevertheless the story must be structured in such a way that it reflects this conditioning.

The pace of the story must be adroitly juggled. Balance the amount of description by using proper proportions of long and short descriptive passages. Intersperse healthy doses of dialogue and action so that descriptions are welcomed back as old friends, rather than tolerated as dead bores.

Trim excess description that threatens to overwhelm the story and transform it from fiction into a scholarly work of historical detail. Description that does not add depth or meaning to the story, or that does not contribute to the point or the tone of the scene, must be deleted. It doesn't matter how well written the descriptive passage is if it detracts from the story. However, don't throw away that beautiful description. Slip it into your file because one day you will be able to use it in another story.

Dialogue is one of the best ways to break up long descriptive passages and to increase the pace, or the tension, of the story. Whenever a character speaks, it focuses attention on the *action* of the scene, rather than on the scene itself.

When the hero says, "You will regret that, my lady!", there is instant tension. There is an understanding that conflict has begun. The reader is then interested in what happens next, and no longer in a long description of the fire and how its yellow light plays across the mantle and the draperies and highlights the forbidding expression on the hero's face. Description of the scene sets the mood. Descriptive dialogue establishes the level of tension.

Dialogue does not always convey tension, however. In the regency romance, dialogue also breaks up the scene or character description by providing dashes of humor. Recall that the regency romance is usually a "comedy of manners". Funny dialogue helps to define the story's overall atmosphere. It also shows another facet of the relationship between characters.

It is difficult to define humor. What is only faintly humorous to one person may be wildly hilarious to another. I try to inject some light repartee into each book by giving the characters something to marvel at. Usually these exchanges derive their humor from the characters' quirks of personality or are borne out of the circumstances that have brought the characters together. Georgette Heyer was the consummate master at this technique. In her books, some of the repartee is so swift that the reader is dazzled. Again, pacing has a good deal to do with how the dialogue comes off. Repartee is generally composed of short, snappy sentences that positively draw the reader into the fun.

Book titles are another form of description. Sometimes a great title is hit upon before ever the story is thought of. *The Waltzing Widow* was such a title. I loved that title. I kept it in my file until one day the story that fit it came to mind.

The title indicates the type of book or perhaps simply evokes the tone of the story. The good descriptive title presents the story to the potential reader; in the sense that its' purpose becomes dual - that of description and of marketing.

Chapter Ten

MARKETING THE REGENCY ROMANCE

First and foremost, pay attention to the title of the book. Though the original title of a book does not always survive the actual production process, an excellent title often does play a role in garnering an acceptance from a publishing house.

At a writer's conference I once attended, there was a seminar of book distributors, those people who buy from publishers and subsequently offer their purchases in such high-traffic places as supermarkets and airports. These gentlemen had developed a very good idea of what sells to the hurrying public and what does not. The distributors unanimously agreed that, besides the book cover, the first selling point of a book is its title.

One distributor said marketing research had shown that as people walked by the bookstands, their eyes scanned each book for approximately ten seconds.

Ten seconds.

In that span of time, the book cover and/or the title had to grab the passerby's attention enough so that he or she would stop to pick up the book. It was only then that there was the possibility of a sale.

The title is important. It is a marketing tool. It is the first word or words that an editor will read from your manuscript. And make no mistake. The *editor* is your customer. If you can't sell your book to the editor, then you'll never have to worry about whether your book will be able to compete in the marketplace, because it won't be there.

The title must attract attention. The style in which it does so depends on the book's content, or the genre. Thrillers rely on words suggesting tension, such as Tom Clancy's *Clear and Present Danger* or *The Hunt for Red October.* An epic historical relies on words suggesting heroic characters, such as Alexandre Dumas's *The Three Musketeers,* or Morgan Llywelyn's *Lion of Ireland.* Historical romances rely on words suggestive of romance, such as Fern Michaels' *To Taste the Wind* or Jude Deveraux's *Knight in Shinning Armour.*

Regency romances rely on words, or even names, that are evocative of the regency era. Examples: *An Infamous Army* and *Faro's Daughter* by Georgette Heyer; *Memoirs of a Hoyden* by Joan Smith; *The Demon Rake* and *Lord John's Lady* by Gayle Buck; *Eugenia* by Clare Darcy; and *The Gallant Lord Ives* by Emily Hendrickson.

The historical background of the regency is a veritable gold-mine of possible titles. Geographic names (Thames and Avon), place names (London and Bath; the Pavilion; Canterbury), street names (St. James, Bond St., and Mayfair), the names of popular entertainments (Astley's Circus; whist and faro) and dances (waltz and cotillion), political happenings (the Peninsular War; Waterloo; the Cato Street conspiracy) and forms of address (miss, lord, lady, duke, duchess, etc.), are all wonderful sources for inspiration in developing the title that best suits a specific book. Mix some of these with descriptive adjectives or possessive nouns and the title comes alive: *An Infamous Army*; *Lord John's Lady*; *The Gallant Lord Ives.*

The title of the regency romance is actually more important than the cover, compared to other genres which rely as much or more on the cover to sell the book. Regency covers adhere closely to the historical background of the story, so that instantly the book browser knows what sort of book it is. The title of the regency reflects this same evocation.

Since the titles of regency romances are actually evocative of that particular era, these titles can be considered esoteric; meaning, these titles appeal to a specific and often fiercely loyal audience.

As a matter of fact, readers of regency romances often do not read anything else. They read regencies because these stories are fun, upbeat and always have a happy ending. I met an engineer who was on 24-hour emergency call on the Louisiana oil rigs who said that she reads only regencies because she could *count on* a lighthearted entertainment that was in direct contrast to the considerable stress of her job. I also know a lady who reads only regencies because, she said, she liked the wit and the lively interaction between the characters - the story did not rely on bed-hopping to prove there was strong attraction and romance in the offing. These are two very different women, but both have found regencies to suit their individual tastes.

The point is that the regency genre is one of the steadiest in the marketplace. Publishing, like nearly every other field, goes through cycles. Some years historicals sell like hotcakes; other years it is spy-catchers that consistently top the best-selling list. The regency romance, because it is a small category and because it has such a very loyal and steady audience, does not have the extreme swings in popularity. Therefore, regencies consistently sell.

That is the up side. The down side is that since the regency romance is a smaller category, it will not receive the big advertising dollars from the publishing house; nor will it ever become a word-of-mouth overnight bestseller. Therefore, the monetary returns for a regency writer are much less than what a writer of glitz or mainstream may expect.

However, the possibilities of publication are greater in the regency category than in many other categories simply because of these marketing realities. Publishing houses are always looking for those "big sellers" and the odds of placing a glitz or mainstream book with a publisher run very high against the writer. But several publishers bring out regencies and, though there is competition in the field, there is far more room to carve out a niche, too.

Some of the publishers who currently have regency lines are Harlequin Regency, New American Library (Signet imprint), Walker & Company, Avon Books, Zebra Books, Fawcett, Ballantine, Pocket, St. Martin's Press, and Pinnacle. For a real bird's-eye look at all of the publishers available for this, or any other particular category, browse your nearest bookstore. Do not forget the Christian bookstores. Recently I visited one and was very interested to note an entire rack of fiction offered that ran the gamut from contemporary and historical romance to young adult and fantasy. Pick up a current copy of the *LMP* (*Literary Market Place*) at your local library. The *LMP* has the publishers' upcoming title lists in it, as well as other information. It is a worthwhile research source to consult to find out if your particular title has already been used or to see what sort of competition there might be for your particular type of book.

The addresses to these publishers can be found in the *LMP*_or the *Writer's Market*, (a big annual reference book of book publishers, trade journals, magazines, greeting card companies and more). The writer's guidelines that each publisher prefers to have followed are readily available for an SASE (self-addressed stamped envelope).

The guidelines for the regency romance are fairly consistent except for differences in length requirements. For example, Harlequin Regency requires a manuscript of 65,000 words, New American Library requires 75,000 words for their Signet imprint and 125,000 to 150,000 words for their Superregencies, while Avon Books requires 100,000 words.

Common sense will tell you that selling an editor on your book depends on a good title and a good story. However, appearance is also vitally important. A fellow regency writer told me that when she participates as a judge for the Romance Writers of America competition, she is immediately more interested in a clean and easily readable manuscript than in one that is poorly typed or smudged. The stories may be comparable in all respects, but the clean manuscript will automatically receive a more favorable reading. This doesn't seem quite fair. However, it is realistic to recognize this very human response. Appearance matters.

The publishers' guidelines will usually include something about manuscript preparation. The *Writer's Market* always has an in-depth article on manuscript mechanics and how to prepare a manuscript for submission. Another source for learning how to put a manuscript together are writers' magazines, which regularly run features on the subject.

Since there are readily available sources that detail exactly how to prepare a manuscript for preparation, I won't go into an in-depth discussion of it here. I will mention a few things, however. An important point to remember is that the manuscript should be on 8 1/2" x 11" white bond, double-spaced, and in an ordinary typescript. Editors will not read single-spaced material in all caps or an odd typescript that they have to decipher. The editor has a stack of manuscripts on her desk, and several more on the floor, that she must go through as quickly as possible. Her eyes are far less strained by a clean, double-spaced manuscript that is easy to read. She will prefer to read that story than one that is hard on her eyes.

If you use a computer, be aware that most publishing houses will not accept a dot-matrix print-out. The resolution of a dot-matrix printer is not as good as that of a daisy-wheel or, even better, a laser printer; therefore, dot-matrix is very hard on the editor's eyes in a 300-or-more page manuscript. Dot-matrix also does not copy as well, which is a definite disadvantage in the production stage of readying a manuscript for publication.

Another marketing tool for your manuscript is the cover letter that will accompany it. This letter should be addressed to a particular editor rather than "The Editor" because a name increases the odds of your manuscript getting where it should go quicker. The difference can be equated to what you get in your own box, those envelopes addressed to you personally and those directed to "Occupant". Which do *you* read first? The editor's name can usually be found in the *Writer's Market*, the *LMP*, or in market listings in writer's magazines. If not, or if you want to be certain to have the latest editor's name for your particular category (editors are notorious for job-hopping), simply call the publisher and ask the receptionist.

Once you have the editor's name, it is time to write a sales pitch for your manuscript. In the first paragraph, tell the editor why you are writing to her - you have written or are in the process of writing a book. Give the title of your book and the category or area that it fits.

In the second paragraph, introduce yourself. Tell the editor about any professional publishing credits that you might have. If you have none, then tell her about any special training or life experiences or interests that have something to do with the type of book that you are submitting. These can range from on-the-job experiences to education, or can be simply a private fascination. One writer I know inherited a collection of books on the regency period, and that is what inspired her to write a regency romance. This writer took a previously unknown area of knowledge and forged it into a published novel.

The third paragraph wraps up the letter. Thank the editor for her time and for her consideration of your submission. Courtesy goes far in impressing an editor of a writer's professionalism.

In its entirety, the cover letter is not more than a page in length. The editor will look more kindly on a submission that has come with a straight-forward and polite cover letter that is mercifully brief, also.

The days in which the writer was required to send an entire manuscript to an editor are past. Today, because of time considerations and of postage costs, it is much more sensible to send a cover letter with a synopsis and partial. Time-wise, the writer does not necessarily need to write the entire book (which is usually at least a two-year proposition for a first novel) in order to have a good grasp for the story, and so sending out a synopsis and partial makes good sense. The writer can test the market waters before expending all of that time and sweat and blood and tears.

A synopsis and partial also makes good sense because months can pass before a publisher will get back to the writer about a submission. The reasons for such horrible delays sometimes have nothing whatsoever to do with the writer's work. One submission I made came back over a year after I had mailed it out, and only then because I wrote to ask that it be returned. As it turned out, the synopsis and partial was never even read by an editor in all that time because the publishing house was in the process of being absorbed by a larger house and the ordinary business of sifting through unsolicited submissions had been suspended. Fortunately, I had already been accepted by another publishing house so that the failure of this particular submission did not really bother me.

This brings up another important point. Do not depend upon one submission. Otherwise you will spend the time until you hear from the publisher biting your nails and see-sawing between hope and despair that your submission will make it. Once a submission is mailed out, get to work on something else immediately. You'll feel far happier.

Another good argument in favor of the synopsis and partial is the difference in time it takes for an editor to read an entire 300-page-or-more manuscript compared to a synopsis and partial. An editor can quickly size up the potential of a proposed book from a good synopsis and partial. She doesn't need the other 230 pages to convince her.

Nothing needs to be said about the cost of postage. A 300-page manuscript will cost more to mail than will a synopsis and partial that is less than a third of that size. If your proposal must be sent out several times before it finds a home, your postage expenditure to mail the full manuscript quickly becomes incredibly hefty.

The synopsis is double-spaced, as is the partial, and usually runs approximately eight pages. Some editors prefer to see more. The synopsis details the action of the novel from beginning to end and introduces the editor to the main characters and the main plot, along with any secondary characters and sub-plots that may be important to the denouement of the story or its depth. The partial consists of the first 50 to 75 pages of the actual manuscript, which roughly divides out into the first four to six chapters of the book. Here again, it is editor or publishing house preference on how long the chapters run. Most houses prefer ten or twelve pages to the chapter; others, as many as 20 pages.

Another important thing to remember when submitting any manuscript, whether full book-length, a synopsis and partial, or a simple query letter, is to include an SASE. Without the self-addressed stamped envelope, the editor will often not send back your submission if it is rejected because the publisher does not want to foot the bill for the postage. Many publishers receive thousands of submissions a year, most of which will be rejected for one reason or another. It would be a punitive cost of doing business for the publisher to pay the postage for all of the returns.

Successful marketing of any manuscript relies on certain requirements; that is, clean and consistent preparation, a good title and story, a publishing house that publishes the particular category that the book fits into, and a particular editor's name which will hopefully generate expedient handling. These requirements can successfully be met by the writer.

Other factors are often beyond the writer's control.

If the publisher's publishing list has already been set for two or three years in advance..

If your book does not quite fit the slant of the category that the publisher is evolving..

If the publisher is in the process of being taken over by another company..

If there is a rivalry between house imprints and the one that loses undergoes trimming of staff or even fade-out..

If the editor that you sent your book to has suddenly taken a hike in the last week..

If the editor who reads your proposal has been in an auto accident and your heroine's surname is Youngblood..

Then you have a rejection.

All of these scenarios are true. With one exception, they have all happened to me. Writing is one thing. Getting published is quite another, and is by far the craziest half of the business.

Try to insulate yourself as much as possible against these kinds of rejections. The *LMP* prints the publishers' upcoming lists, as well as ads on particular books. Check to see if any of the scheduled books sounds too close in storyline to yours. See if the title of your book is already being used. If it is, but in a different category, you will probably be able to go ahead and use it. Refer also to *Books in Print* at the local library to see if your title has been used and if so, how long ago. Apparently even if the books are in the same category, the publishers don't mind reusing a title if the books are far enough apart in publication.

Find out by calling the publisher if the publishing list has already been set for the category you are interested in. You will be referred to an editor or an editorial assistant who works with that category. Simply explain that you have in mind a submission for that category and you wondered whether the publishing list was full. If it is full, the editors are not really going to be interested in looking at new manuscripts. It would be a waste of your time to send your proposal to them unless you don't mind waiting months while it sits in their office. It would be a better use of time to find a publisher who is actively setting up their publishing list for the upcoming year or two and who is possibly on the look-out for just your sort of book.

An example to illustrate this particular point is my own experience while at a writers' conference. I listened to a panel of editors outline what their particular houses needed and were looking for. Afterwards, I approached two of the editors about a particular idea that I had, which fit the category that each had said she wanted to see. One editor's eyes slid away from mine while she waited for me to finish. Then she said that her house's publishing schedule was full for the next two years and that the publisher was not buying anything. The lady gave me exactly two sentences. Contrast this with my reception from the other editor, who asked me a couple of questions about the project before she whipped out her business card and told me to call her. She said that her house was even then in the process of deciding what was to go into their publishing schedule for the next two years and she was very interested in seeing what I could work up for her.

The *LMP* will also give you a fair idea about the availability of space on the publisher's publishing schedule. Also look at writers' magazines because their market updates are more recent than those in the *Writer's Market*.

Read several books in your chosen category. Make a note of the publishers that you want to target for submission. You will begin to get a feel for what the publisher has brought out and how the stories may be changing and in what direction. All categories evolve. Regency romances are no different. Some publishers are looking for more sensuality in their regency line. Some will not accept a story in which the heroine masquerades in boy's clothing. Some prefer that the story remain entirely in England, or even London, while other publishers may allow the regency heroine to travel abroad. Some publishers tend to bring out stories that are entirely lighthearted while others want graver aspects explored within the context of the story.

Make as certain as you can that the editor you are submitting to is in residence at the publishing house, either through writers' magazine updates or by placing a phone call.

The rest of the possible rejections are catch-as-can. There are as many reasons for rejection as there are stars in the sky, and most cannot be anticipated or controlled in any way by the writer. Just do the best you possibly can.

Whenever you do receive a rejection, do not totally despair. It is natural to feel depressed at receiving a rejection for something that you have poured your heart and soul into, but look at the rejection. It could be telling you something positive, too. A form letter rejection with no personal annotation from the editor is by far the most discouraging. If, however, that same form letter has scrawled at the bottom a brief "Sorry.", and the editor's initial, then take heart. The editor liked something about the proposal, but due to whatever extenuating circumstance, such as those outlined above, an acceptance cannot be forthcoming.

If the editor takes the time to actually type a real letter, especially if it outlines particular problems with your story, then realize that the door is not firmly closed against you. Work on the problems that the editor has mentioned and resubmit your proposal, with a cover letter thanking the editor for her previous constructive criticisms and that you have incorporated those suggestions into your revised submission. You will at least get a second reading and maybe this time around you will receive a letter that is cautiously encouraging. It is still not an acceptance, but you have been thrown a line. What you do with that line, whether you firmly grasp it with the intention to make the most of it, or you let it fall because you feel too dejected to even try, is up to you.

It has been my experience that once you have touched the editor in some way with your writing, it is often very worthwhile to keep knocking on that same editor's door. Eventually, if your revisions begin to find the direction that the editor is looking for, the door opens and you are invited inside.

If you do not receive any further encouragement, at least make a note of that editor's name and put it into your file. Editors leap-frog from publishing house to publishing house. In future, at a different publishing house and under different publishing circumstances, the editor who once scribbled "Sorry.", on your submission could very well be the person who is most receptive to your newest proposal.

Chapter Eleven

CONTRACTS, MONEY, AND AGENTS

Most publishing houses are honest in their dealings when contracting with an author. Just as in any other field, however, there are a few that might cross the line. But for the most part, a writer need not be paranoid about getting a bad deal. This does not mean that the publisher will bend over backwards to give every advantage to the writer. The publisher naturally wants as many pieces of the profit pie as the writer is willing to give away. The writer, of course, wants very much to be able to make a nice tidy sum off what has been a long, involved, and often painful, project. In order to cut the very best deal possible, every writer should educate himself or herself in advance of what to expect in the contractual process and what to expect in the contract.

This chapter is about what to expect. However, due to space constraints not every contract clause will be discussed. Please consult other sources for samples of contracts, explanations, and suggestions, as well as professionals in the publishing industry, such as lawyers who specialize in the entertainment field and reputable agents.

When the publishing house contacts you to let you know that it is interested in buying your book, the good news will usually come through a telephone call. Be prepared to be thrown into a state of happy shock.

Be prepared, also, to negotiate. That is the second thing that this telephone call is all about. Whatever you agree to, while still feeling completely dazed, is a binding agreement that will later appear in the written contract. I'd recommend keeping near the telephone a sheet of paper with a list of the items that are the most likely to be discussed in this initial contact. Then when that incredible phone call comes, you will be better able to respond in a business-like manner.

Some terms to familiarize yourself with, and which may or may not be discussed during the first telephone call, follow. First, however, I'd like to make mention of two other things that will and should be touched on during the initial phone call.

One of the first questions that the editor will ask you is whether you have an agent. If you don't, then she will proceed full-steam. If you do, make sure that you do not agree to anything. Instead, tell the editor that you are interested in her offer but you would like to consult with your agent about the specific terms that she is offering before committing yourself. If you do agree to something like a specific advance and later your agent tells you that you could have gotten better, the matter is already settled. You can't go back to the editor with this hindsight and say that you want to renegotiate the advance.

Once the editor has gone over the points that she deems most important to get buttoned up, she will say that the rest of the contract is standard and need not be discussed. At this point the question that you as the writer should ask, whether or not you have an agent, is what the standard contract is for that particular publishing house. You may very well discover that the standard contract contains clauses that can be negotiated to your benefit. Before giving blanket agreement to the "standard contract", request that you be allowed to read the contract in its entirety. If the editor is reluctant to send a copy of the contract to you before you have agreed to it, then pull out your sheet of paper and gently tell the editor that you would like to go over some specific clauses so that you will know what the publishing house's standard contract is all about.

This is scary stuff. You don't want to offend the editor because you fear that she will decide not to take your book after all. You don't want to push too hard for the same reason, especially if you are a first-time author. First-timers are definitely at the worst disadvantage because they fear that this offer is the only one that they will ever get. Also, they do not have a track record and the editor has a legitimate claim to exercising caution when buying a first novel - will it sell well or won't it? However, if the writer has learned something about contracts and what to expect beforehand, then even for the first-timer it is worth the risk to open discussion on those points that are most negotiable.

Of course, if you do have an agent, you don't need to worry so much about taking the chance of souring your possible future working relationship with the editor. The agent gets paid for taking the heat as well as for dishing it out. We'll spend some time on agents in a moment.

Now for the nitty-gritty.

The grant of rights. This is what the publisher is acquiring from the writer and it lists everything. The publisher basically acquires rights for the full term of copyright and for all renewals and extensions of copyright. Copyright lasts for the author's lifetime, plus fifty years. Before any changes are made to it, this grant of rights gives the publisher all rights to your work, including translation rights, world rights, performance rights, and often first serialization rights. The publisher has representatives who will attempt to place these rights. An agent will also work to sell these rights. If you are unagented, then the publisher will likely be better able to place these rights than you are. However, ask the editor to amend the clause so that the rights in question revert to you if the publisher does not place them within 18 months of publication. Then if you do get an agent later, the agent will be able to work on selling the rights for you even after the publisher's representatives have already taken their shot.

The advance. This is how much total money that the publisher agrees to pay the writer in advance against royalties and future earnings (monies earned through subsidiary rights). In other words, the publisher agrees to let you borrow this amount with the expectation that your book will earn enough, or more, to satisfy the loan. If your book fails to earn back the amount advanced to you, then you must return the difference that was not earned to the publisher. The publisher will usually under-estimate the amount of sales that your book will generate, though, so this is not a problem unless the publisher has totally erred in the appeal of your book or does not do a proper job in getting it out to the public.

When the editor calls to tell you of her interest in your book, she already has in mind an advance figure. Advances are worked out using profit-and-loss sheets that take into account sales in that category, production costs, cover costs, royalties, freight costs, etc. The figure is arrived at and the offer is made to you. Sometimes the editor does have some room to negotiate the advance, but keep in mind how the advance was arrived at. No publishing house is going to offer more for an advance than the profit-and-loss sheet estimates that the book will earn back.

The usual advance for a mass market paperback regency written by a first time author is $2,000. This amount will be split into two or three payments over the course of completing the book. The advance for future regencies by the same author will grow at most to about $4,000 per book. I'd guestimate that over the life of a mass market paperback regency romance, it will earn an average of $5,000 to $7,000.

The "life" of the book is approximately two years. However, the book is actually on the bookshelves only 30 to 90 days, depending on the size of the bookstore. Independent bookstores keep titles longer on the shelves than do the chains, which buy in greater volume and therefore must move their inventory faster. The book remains in print, - that is, it can be ordered - for an average of two years after its publication date.

Once the book goes out of print, the writer should remind her editor of the book's existence and ask about the possibility of scheduling a reprint. Reprinting a title breathes new life into its earning potential. Most publishers have regular schedules for reprints of old titles. For instance, New American Library prints three new regency titles and three regency reprints every month of every year.

The payout. This is how the advance will be paid out to the writer. This payout varies depending on the publisher, at what stage of completion the book is in, and the size of the advance.

If the book is complete and requires little editorial work, then the publisher will pay the full amount of the advance upon signing of the contract (meaning approximately four or more weeks before you actually receive the check in the mail). If the book is only partially completed or if in synopsis and partial form, the publisher usually pays an amount with the signing of the contract and the remainder upon completion and acceptance of the book. (Even if the publisher expresses an interest in a synopsis and partial, most publishers want to see a full manuscript from a first-time writer before they are willing to part with any money. Once you have a track record, of course, you will receive advances on the basis of a synopsis and partial alone.)

Some publishers pay in three installments: upon signing of the contract, upon acceptance of half of the book, and upon full completion. The larger the advance, the longer the publisher will want to delay payment. This is understandable from the publisher's viewpoint. Firstly, the publisher wants to be certain that the contracted product (the book) will be completed before they actually invest in it; secondly, the longer the publisher can keep the money, the more investment interest it will earn before it passes out of the publisher's accounts.

The territories. This defines exactly what parts of the world that the publisher has the right to sell the book in. Generally, American publishers want "North American rights", which consist of the United States, Canada, and adjacent territories, and "open market", which includes sales in the English language anywhere outside the British Commonwealth. "World English rights" include the British Commonwealth (Britain, Ireland, Scotland, Wales, Australia, New Zealand, and smaller territories). American publishers usually don't sell the book themselves in these markets, but instead license the rights to British publishers. "World rights, all languages" includes all of the above, plus translations into other languages. An agent will try to limit the publishers' acquisition of rights to publication in the United States, the Philippines, and Canada, and for English language publication only.

The royalty. This is the percentage amount of the retail cover price paid to the writer for every copy of the book sold. Make a note that the royalty comes off of the retail price. I have heard of the rare contract in which the royalty is derived from the wholesale price of the book. Never sign such a contract, because the wholesale price is what the bookstore pays the publisher and that is 40% to 55% off the retail, or cover, price of the book. Using a 6% royalty, it is the difference in being paid $.24 per copy or $.11 per copy for a book that sells for $3.95 retail. The royalty derived from the wholesale price of the book is less than half what the writer could get from the royalty that is derived from the retail price of the book.

Royalty percentages differ depending upon the type of book and the standard practice at the publishing house. Hardcover royalties are usually 10% for the first 5,000 copies sold, 12 1/2% for the next 5,000 copies and 15% thereafter. Royalties for trade paperbacks - those large 6" X 9" paperbacks - start from 6% to 7 1/2% and may go up to 9% or 10% at a certain point in sales. Mass market paperback royalties, where most of the regency romances fall, range from 6% to 8% and usually go up to 10% at some point in sales.

Again, there is the rare contract that grants less than the publishing industry standard royalties to a writer. I have heard of a writer who accepted a 3% royalty, either because she did not know what the standard royalty was for a mass market paperback or because she was absolutely desperate to be published. If it was the latter reason, this lady made a truly grave error quite aside from the unnecessary loss of income. Once a writer has accepted less than the standard, it is very difficult to renegotiate future works at a higher percentage because the publisher already sees that particular writer as a push-over. As for the desperation angle, any book that one publisher thinks is good enough to publish will be of interest to other publishers as well. Publishers don't publish books that they know won't make a profit. So again, do not sign a contract that outlines less than the publishing industry's standard.

Royalties are accounted for and are paid semi-annually. This schedule will appear in the contract. A royalty statement breaks down the number of bookstore orders, reports any returns, adds up what each title has earned, subtracts any advance amounts, and, finally, gives the total earnings for all titles. A check for the total earnings is attached to the royalty statement.

The term "returns" refers to the bookstores' right to return any unsold copies to the publisher. Obviously, then, a book ordered is not necessarily a book sold. The publishing house hedges its bets against returns by subtracting the anticipated number of returns against the actual bookstore orders. Therefore the royalty statement received by the writer can be somewhat deceiving. If the publisher has erred in anticipating the number of returns, then future royalty statements must be amended to reflect the true figure. This explains how a book that has been out of print for two or more years can still be earning royalties - the publisher overestimated the number of returns and thereafter sends already-earned royalties to the writer in dribs and drabs until the account is finally balanced.

The delivery date. This is the date that a writer agrees to deliver the manuscript on. The publisher usually gives the first-time writer at least ten months to finish and deliver the manuscript. On a subsequent book, the publisher and the writer might agree on a much shorter turnaround. Obviously, the more books that can be written and published in a certain length of time, the greater the profit for both publisher and writer.

This factor brings up an interesting point. A writer who regularly puts out a book every six months or so will build up an audience that will recognize her name and who will be conditioned to look for her books. A writer who publishes a book every other year will not build an audience. Each book will only be a fresh introduction for the writer. When name recognition begins to work for a writer, the competition's sales with the same audience will automatically be cut down. (This is true of mass-market paperbacks. For someone like Stephen King or James Michener, a book every other year is hardly a drawback.)

The delivery date agreed upon is not necessarily written in stone. Depending on where the publisher places the book on the publishing schedule, there is usually room for compromise. Usually a book is in production, (the time from which the completed manuscript is accepted to the time that the book is published), a minimum of nine months. If the book is scheduled for publication eighteen months later, then the writer who has a personal emergency or a period of writer's block or whatever will usually find the editor willing to grant a time extension in getting the book done. On the other hand, if the book is scheduled for publication in exactly ten months, then the writer is faced with the possibility of having her book bumped from its place on the publishing schedule. The book may then have to wait as long as two years before it sees the light of day. The book does not start earning royalties until it is published and sold, so this is extremely detrimental to the writer's bank account.

Subsidiary rights. The various subsidiary rights include paperback rights, book club rights, foreign language translations, film rights, audio tape rights, etc. The proceeds from the licensing of these rights are divided between the publishing house and the writer. For British and foreign language rights, the split is usually 50/50 up to 80/20, writer's favor. Paperback, book club and second serial rights are almost always split 50/50. In some of the larger book contracts the rights lean more in the writer's favor once a certain amount is earned.

Book length. The number of words required in the book runs in the thousands. Depending on the publishing house, this length will differ. We've already briefly touched on this topic while discussing the requirements set out in the publishers' guidelines. Regency romances can run anywhere from 65,000 words (Harlequin) to 75,000 words (New American Library-Signet imprint) to 100,000 words (Avon).

This brings up a related point. There is a contractual clause called Author's Next Work, or the option clause, which basically states that any future book-length work done by the author, whether under his or her own name or a pseudonym, must be offered to the same publisher before submission to any other publisher. It is a good idea to revise this clause to read that any future *Regency* work of (here include the specific wordage required by the publisher) length will be offered to the same publisher, etc., etc.

The reason for this is that often a writer wants to write in more than one category. If the clause stands as it is, the writer has no choice but to submit all of her work to the same publisher. Should the writer then be reduced to the one market for all of her various types of work? Where is the competition in that? Also, by adding the specific word length into the clause, the writer can do regencies for more than one publisher. I know of a writer who at one time was placing regencies with three different publishing houses at once - one at 65,000 words, one at 75,000 words, and the last at 150,000 words. She still writes for two publishing houses, the third having since faded out their regency line. This writer's income is quite nicely rounded out because she has been able to do this.

These are just some of the items that are found in a contract. These are also points that are the most likely to be haggled over. Since I have never had an agent, I am myself still learning about contracts and what is negotiable and what is not. I try to learn as much as I can so that in future each contract that I sign is just a little bit more advantageous. It is often difficult to play the businesswoman. A writer essentially creates the product. In other types of business, the creative expert is usually not also the marketing expert. But a writer must learn to be both, if a real career is to be built.

The bottom line is that a writer must educate himself or herself. Read books about writing and publishing. Some good sources are *How To Get Happily Published* by Judith Appelbaum and Nancy Evans (Harper & Row, 1988), *Negotiating A Book Contract* by Mark Levine (Moyer Bell Limited, Colonial Hill, Mt. Kisco, New York 10549), and *How To Be Your Own Literary Agent* by Richard Curtis (Houghton Mifflin, 1984).

Read magazines for writers, such *Writer's Digest* and *The Writer*. The Writer's Digest Book Club, which is advertised in *Writer's Digest* magazine and sends out catalogues to subscribers to the magazine, has an entire listing of useful books dealing with writing and the publishing industry. In addition, writers' magazines often feature articles on contract negotiation that are written by professionals in the publishing field, including editors and agents as well as savvy writers.

Attend seminars given by people who have actually published. Those who haven't published do not have a pool of personal experience to draw from. Personal experience inevitably tempers all theory and makes it much more applicable. Many times a university or local public school have guest speakers who come in to tell what they know and have learned about writing and getting published. Community Education classes are also another possible source for finding out information. These types of talks are usually inexpensive to attend.

If you can afford to, go to writers' conferences and talk to writers who have been, or are trying to be, published. The energy flying around is enormous, and it is as invigorating for the published writers as it is for the aspiring writer. You will learn more from listening and asking questions than you could ever learn otherwise. Don't be afraid to talk to a writer whose name you recognize. These people are genuinely interested in talking about their craft and are some of the nicest people you will ever associate with. Certainly there are a few inflated egos, but as a rule, writers are pretty approachable as long as they are not dogged.

Writers' conferences are held all over the country and are sponsored by local and regional writers' groups, by universities, by national writers' groups, and by commercial interests. Often the conferences are advertised in writers' magazines or in writers' groups newsletters. Some are inexpensive. Some are not.

When I became a member of my own regional writers' group, the Austin Writers' League, I was amazed at the sophistication and variety of seminars that were offered to members. The seminars often pulled in big names in both publishing and writing. Tapes of the seminars are available to those who cannot attend in person. (For information, write the AWL at 1501 West 5th St. #109, Austin, Texas 78703.) I am certain that other regional groups across the country are just as effective in bringing information and encouragement to their members. I strongly recommend that every writer seek out like individuals, if only to hear the latest news on different publishers. At best, you will have a built-in support group who understands the challenges associated with writing.

Several pages ago I promised to discuss agents. Having an agent is a personal preference as well as a business decision. If you don't have the faintest idea of where to start looking for a publisher and you really don't feel that you will ever learn enough to be able to make a good decision, or you really cringe from the thought of negotiating a contract, then probably you might feel more comfortable dealing through an agent. If you think that you can learn the ropes as you go along and also prefer to handle your business yourself, then don't bother with an agent.

While it is true that many publishing houses now prefer to deal through an agent, who can be trusted to send them submissions well-suited to their market needs, there are still many opportunities for getting a foot in the door without an agent's prior introduction. I have even found that some publishing houses which state in the *Writer's Market* that they prefer to see agented material will still give the unrepresented writer a fair shot.

An agent will usually charge 15% of the writer's earnings as his or her commission. (A few still adhere to the old standard, which was 10%.) This commission is on the initial sale to the publisher as well as on any subsidiary rights that may later be sold. In addition, the agent will sometimes charge back such costs as telephone calls made on behalf of the writer and making xerox copies of the writer's work that will be used for submission to selected publishers that might be expected to express an interest in the manuscript.

Many agents now charge a reading fee, which can range anywhere from $50 to $500 or more. This is up-front money that is usually not returned to the writer. The reading fee is often considered to be a worthwhile investment by those fortunate writers who later see their work published. However, this is also the area where many aspiring writers have been burned. I have a friend who sent a total of more than $2,000 in reading fees to various agents with never a sale to show for it. One agent, she discovered, never even sent out her proposal but let it sit in the file for months. Another lady told me about an agent who took on as many new clients as possible, collected the reading fees, and thereafter kept herself incommunicado from her clients. This agent subsequently lost some of her clients because she also apparently did very little to place their work. There are many very reputable and trustworthy agents in the industry, but those who are not malign honest agents by their actions.

How do you find an agent? Agents are listed in the *LMP* and advertise in various writers' magazines. You can write those who express an interest in seeing material for the category in which you are writing. Agents attend writing seminars and conferences to speak about the publishing industry. One reason they are there is to develop new client relationships. Many agents, however, are not interested in writers who do not already have a track record or who are writing for categories in which there are not big bucks to be made. (Glitz and mainstream earn the highest monies of any other categories.) I have a great deal of respect for the agent who will be honest enough to tell a writer up-front, before ever a reading fee might change hands, that she will not represent the writer because the writer is not yet earning enough to make representation worthwhile. Agents want to make a living just like anyone else and even if they are looking for new clients, they prefer to take on those who will make them the most money in commissions or, at the very least, those who have already proven that they can write a marketable book.

I think the best possible way to find an agent that is reputable and that will best suit your particular needs and personality is to talk to other writers. They will tell you about their experiences with different agents and often will give you the name of their own agents, with permission to use their name as the person who recommended the agent to you. It always helps to know someone who knows someone. (The same goes for editors, by the way. Be sure to let the editor who receives your proposal know if there was someone, like a recognized writer or another editor, who recommended that you send your proposal to her. It warms up the editor's interest.)

Basically, what an agent does is take over the every-day tasks associated with writing. This includes contract negotiations, seeking out new markets, encouraging the writer, keeping a running account of earnings, and running interference between writer and editor. The agent's job is to market the writer's book for the very best contract terms possible, which frees the writer to do what he or she does best - write. Depending on his or her own personal style, the agent can be very aggressive or apply a gentler approach to the job.

This last factor is important to the writer's relationship with the agent. A writer who is intimidated by her agent's aggressive personality will not be happy and will be unable to express fully what she expects of the agent. On the other hand, a writer who is aggressive by nature will be impatient with an agent whose style is more relaxed. Either of these situations will not lead to a good working relationship or to better sales. This is another reason that finding an agent through other writers is a good idea. You will get a fair notion of the agent's personality and working style before ever an agreement is made between the two of you, and I think this can be something of a safeguard against disillusionment for both parties.

This chapter is a very general overview of what to expect in contracts, money, and agents. It is actually just a starting point, to alert you that there is so much more to learn. It will be to your benefit to continue to educate yourself and to listen to what others have experienced. There is no one best path to publication. Every writer has a slightly different story, some funny, some bittersweet. Absorb them all and learn, so that when your turn comes you can make the decisions that are the best for you.

Appendix

Research References

The following are a few suggested references to consult in the course of researching a regency romance. Most I have consulted myself and others are suggestions by other regency writers. Many of these references will be readily available through a large public library or, at the very least, through inter-library loan. This list is by no means to be considered definitive. See the suggested topic headings in the chapter on research for further reference leads.

Elements of Style by Strunk and White (MacMillan and Company) - Buy this 78-page book. It is an absolute necessity for proper grammatical usage and punctuation in writing.

Oxford English Dictionary - Dates the first known use of each word it defines so that the writer can cull out words in the manuscript that were not in use during the regency era.

Roget's Thesaurus - A reference of synonyms and antonyms that is invaluable.

*   *   *   *

FASHION:

Costume 1066-1966 by Peacock (Thames & Hudson)

Patterns of Fashion by Janet Arnold (MacMillan/Drama Books)

A Handbook of English Clothing in the 19th Century by C. Willett & Phyllis Cunnington (London Faber 1967)

English Costume in the Nineteenth Century by James Laver

Connoisseur Period Guides: The Regency Period by R. & Ramsey Edwards (NY: Reyna 1957)

Costume Reference Series #5: The Regency by Marion Sichel (Plays, Inc. 1978)

Dress and Undress: A History of Women's Underwear by Elizabeth Ewing (Reissue by Bibliophile 1978)

*   *   *   *

GENERAL OVERVIEW:

The Prince of Pleasure and His Regency by J. B. Priestley (Harper & Row 1969)

The Age of Elegance by Arthur Bryant (Harper 1950)

Regency London by Stella Margetson (Praeger Publishers, Inc. 1971)

The Age of Elegance by Sir Arthur Bryant (Harper & Bros. 1950)

Our Tempestuous Day by Carolly Erickson (NY: Morrow 1986)

The Age of Illusion: Manners and Morals 1750-1848 by James Laver (NY: David McKay 1972)

The Congress Dances by Susan Mary Alsop (NY: Harper & Row 1984)

Gilded Butterflies: The Rise and Fall of the London Season by Philippa Pullar (Hamish Hamilton 1978)

*   *   *   *

MEMOIRS, ETC.:

Memoirs of Harriette Wilson

Reminiscences (Vols. I & II) of Captain R. H. Gronow

Life in London by Pierce Egan (1821)

Mrs. Hurst Dancing and Other Scenes from Regency Life 1812-1823, published by Victor Gollancz, 1981

Social England Under the Regency by John Ashton (1895)

The Regency Reference Book by Emily Hendrickson, publication date to be announced

*   *   *   *

MAGAZINES AND NEWSPAPERS:
(These will be on microfiche.)
The Morning Chronicle

The Morning Post

The Gentleman's Magazine

The Lady's Magazine

The Mirror of Fashion

*   *   *   *

DISREPUTABLE SORTS AND SLANG:

Thieves' Kitchen by Donald A. Low (J. M. Dent 1982)

The 1811 Dictionary of the Vulgar Tongue: A Dictionary of Buckish Slang, University Wit and Pickpocket Eloquence (Bibliophile Books)

          *   *   *   *

SPECIFIC TOPICS:

Coaching Days and Coaching Ways by W. Outram Tristam (Bracken 1985)

Sporting Prints by F. L. Wilder (Thames &Hudson 1974)

Shopping in Style by Alison Adburgham (Thames &Hudson 1979)

Shops and Shopping 1800-1914 by Alison Adburgham (George Allen & Unwin 1964)

The History of Gambling in England by John Ashton (1800, reprinted Burt Franklin 1968)

Inns, Ales, and Drinking Customs of Old England by Frederick W. Hackwood (Bracken 1985)

The Story of English Furniture by Bernard Price (British Broadcasting Corp. 1978)

Royal Heritage: The Story of Britain's Royal Builders and Collectors by J. H. Plumb and Huw Wheldon (Chancellor Press 1977)

          *   *   *   *

BIOGRAPHIES:

Lives of the Georgian Age 1714-1837, edited by William Gould (Barnes & Noble 1978)

George IV, Regent and King by Christopher Hibbert (Readers Union 1975)

The Rise and Fall of a Regency Dandy: The Life and Times of Scrope Berdmore Davies by T. A. J. Burnett (Little, Brown 1981)

*　　　*　　　*　　　*

PLACE DESCRIPTIONS:

London in the Nineteenth Century by Thomas Shepherd

A History of London by Robert Gray (Dorset Press 1978)

The Spas of England by Peter J. Neville Havins (Robert Hale & Co. 1876)

The City of Bath by Barry Cunliffe (Yale University Press 1986)

Villages of England by Brian Bailey (Harmony Books 1984)

The Illustrated Counties of England, edited by James Bishop (Facts on File 1980)